YANKEE IN THE WHITE HOUSE

John Quincy Adams

Born: July 11, 1767
Died: February 23, 1848

♥

The Adams family gave America many distinguished figures—but John Quincy Adams towers
above them all. In an incredible career spanning
the nation's first fifty years, when its survival and
destiny hung in delicate balance, he served as foreign minister, ambassador, senator, Secretary of
State, President, and finally as congressman. He
acted in all these posts with an unselfish devotion
to duty as rare as it is inspiring; few men have
ever matched his ability and patriotism. John
Quincy Adams stands as an embodiment of those
qualities of heart and mind which preserved and
shaped our United States.

BOOKS BY MARY HOEHLING

THADDEUS LOWE
America's One-Man Air Corps

GIRL SOLDIER AND SPY
Sarah Emma Edmundson

YANKEE IN THE WHITE HOUSE
John Quincy Adams

Yankee in the White House

John Quincy Adams

★★

by Mary Hoehling

Julian Messner, Inc. New York

Published by Julian Messner, Inc.
8 West 40th Street, New York 18

Published simultaneously in Canada
by The Copp Clark Publishing Co. Limited

Second Printing, 1963

Printed in the United States of America
Library of Congress Catalog Card No. 63-8654

★★★

Acknowledgments

For manuscripts and letters used in the preparation of this biography, I wish to thank Mr. L. H. Butterfield, librarian in charge of the Adams Papers at the Massachusetts Historical Society in Boston, and his secretary, Marjorie E. Sprague; Miss Jeanne Spence of the American Antiquarian Society, Worcester, Massachusetts; and Mrs. Dorothy Eaton and Mr. de Porry of the Manuscript Division, Library of Congress.

For invaluable advice and patient editing, I wish to thank my husband, A. A. Hoehling.

Special mention should be made of historian Samuel Flagg Bemis' comprehensive two-volume biography of John Quincy Adams. This masterly interpretation and analysis of historical events in which John Quincy Adams played a leading role has been an indispensable aid to me.

★★★

Foreword

The world of John Quincy Adams was, like that of today, a restless, changing world. He was born a British subject in the Massachusetts Colony in 1767. Before he was ten years old, revolution had made him a citizen of the world's newest nation.

The story of John Quincy Adams is the story of the growing-up of the world's first true republic. It is the story of his remarkable half-century of service to that republic—a record rarely duplicated.

This is the record of a proud man who was honored with his country's highest office, then continued to serve her in a humbler post. It is the record of an uncompromising patriot who fought an often lonely battle for independence, for union, and for those human rights which are the keystone of democracy.

★★

Contents

1

★★★★★★★★★★★★★★★★★★★★★ 1 ★★★★★★★★★★★★★★★★★★★★★

The Muster Bell

▼

John Quincy Adams lay on his stomach in the stubbly grass of Braintree Common and watched his Uncle Elihu put the local militia through its paces. The motley group of men and boys straggled unevenly up and down the field, shirttails flapping saucily in the breeze. Whenever Captain Adams ordered an about face or a column right or left, some gawky lad would stumble off in the wrong direction, bringing loud guffaws from his fellows.

"All right, take a rest," called Elihu, "then we'll try it again." He sighed, pushing his sandy hair back from his perspiring forehead.

Johnny wriggled his skinny little body in the hot sun. His sharp features were tense with impatience. There was nothing he liked better than a parade. Until this summer of 1774, his father had kept a home and law office in Boston near the Common where British regulars were quartered. His nurse had taken him often to watch them drill. He had spent hours practicing the maneuvers, snapping out the orders to himself, sometimes lugging his father's empty musket, though it was as big as he.

So now, though only seven, Johnny was painfully aware that the homespun spectacle before him hardly compared with the measured tread and precise movements of the Redcoats. Still, the clanging of the muster bell never failed to bring him running down the Shore Road close behind the farm hands. He had made it his job to carry water from the well, though it took all his strength to hoist the wooden bucket, and half the water slopped out before he reached the Common. Day after day they marched, yet seemed to make no progress.

"Pretty ragged, aren't they," remarked Peter Adams, Johnny's younger uncle, as he flopped on the grass beside his nephew.

"They're good shots, even with those old muskets," Johnny conceded. "But surely they're no match for the British!"

Peter Adams stared thoughtfully at the men, sprawled like himself on the grass or slurping water thirstily from the bucket Johnny had brought. Two brawny boys had started a scuffle and a roar went up when someone hurled a dipper of water at the wrestlers.

"They'll fight if need be, Johnny," mused Uncle Peter. "Shiny buckles and dressed parade lines aren't all that make a soldier."

War seemed remote from this sun-drenched world. Yet eleven miles to the north, across the bay, Boston chafed under military rule, its port closed as punishment for a rebellious prank. The Massachusetts Colony had lost all semblance of self-rule since Boston men, dressed as Mohawk Indians, had thrown the cargo of three tea ships into the harbor rather than pay duty on the tea.

Far to the south, the Virginia Colony denounced Britain's action against Massachusetts. The rights of all the colonies were "menaced," Virginia's assembly declared, and called for a Continental Congress. In June, Johnny's father, John Adams, had closed his law office in Boston and sent his wife, Abigail, with the children back to the farm in Braintree, while he rode off to Philadelphia as one of the delegates from Massachusetts.

Except for the excitement of the muster, this summer was no different from any other Johnny remembered. He and his big sister Abigail—whom they called "Nabby" to distinguish her from her mother—with baby brother Charles in tow, followed the farm hands over rocky fields that had been tilled by an Adams since 1636. The cool salt breeze wafted across Penn's Hill, beckoning the children from the hot fields to comb the beaches for shells or treasured flotsam from some unfortunate ship.

Sometimes after a storm, huge timbers were washed onto the beach, and the children would drag them to the woodpile in the kitchen shed. A well-stocked woodshed was important when the wind whistled through the cracks of the old farmhouse and snow drifted to the eaves. This year, with the Port of Boston under blockade, ample supplies would be more important than ever.

Through the autumn, the Adams family, like farmers all over the colony, labored to bring in the harvest. Onions and corn were hung from the rafters in the stone basement, and the pungence of stewing fruits and spices permeated the house. The aroma was tantalizing to Johnny, and seemed to reach him even in the farthest field.

He loved best of all the hours of reading and study beside the hearth. The crackling logs accompanied little Charles as he spelled out the words in his horn book, while baby Thomas gurgled contentedly in his cradle. Nabby's brown hair gleamed golden in the light from the fire beneath a row of pewter spoons hanging proudly on the wall.

Had it not been for the British occupation, John Quincy would have entered the Latin School in Boston this fall. His father thought him far too clever for a country schoolmaster, so his mother was teaching him with the occasional help of her cousin John Thaxter, who was also John Adams' law clerk. They found it difficult to satisfy the boy's hungry mind. In addition to his regular lessons, his mother had him read Rollin's *Ancient History* aloud to her and Nabby as they went about their kitchen duties.

"He hardly hesitates over the longest words," Abigail Adams wrote her husband proudly, "and has almost caught up with Nabby in the *Latin Accidence* and *Took's French Grammar*, though your daughter is a quick student herself!"

Before the snow flew, John Adams rode home from the first Continental Congress. Thankful to return to his own fireside, he had no illusion that the reunion with Britain, for which Congress still worked, could ever be effected.

"I am convinced," he told his family, "that America will support the Massachusetts Colony or perish with her. The word 'independence' cannot yet be spoken aloud in Congress, but it will be soon. It is in the people's hearts."

All semblance of peace melted with the snow. At midmorning of Wednesday, April 19, 1775, a messenger galloped down the Shore Road shouting the call to arms. Johnny stood beside his father as horse and rider drank from their well. British soldiers, the messenger reported, had marched out from Boston that dawn to seize ammunition stored at Concord.

"Some say they meant to arrest your cousin Sam Adams and John Hancock who was stayin' with the Reverend at Lexington—but they was warned and got away."

A small group of Colonial militia had been waiting for the

British on Lexington Common. Shots were fired and several citizens had fallen.

"Murdered on their own doorsteps, ye might say!"—the messenger shook his fist—"while them bloody Redcoats marched along towards Concord tootlin' on their damnable fifes—beggin' your pardon, ma'am!" He tipped his hat to Mrs. Adams who had just appeared in the doorway, "—and singin' 'Yankee Doodle,' if ye please!"

Then the rider was on his horse and off down the road, shouting at the next farm: "To arms!"

All across the countryside, church bells clanged while messengers fanned out to the west and south to spread the alarm. The hated British were on the march!

In moments, Abigail Adams had the housemaids bustling in the kitchen preparing soup while she plunged to her elbows into the biggest pile of dough Johnny had ever seen. Nabby, with Charles in tow, had gone into the garden for more vegetables for the soup.

Out on the road, the sound of voices testified that the militia was gathering.

"Johnny, fetch some water from the well and set it here on the doorsill," Uncle Elihu called through the window.

The road was already full of men. Now Johnny understood why they had been nicknamed "Minutemen." They seemed to have sprung from the earth fully armed like the army that had grown from dragon seed in the old fairy tale. In no time they filled their canteens and marched off toward Boston. Pride and fear fought for first place in Johnny's heart as he watched them until they were out of sight. Those were his friends and neighbors, uncles and cousins—some boys hardly older than he—marching off to fight a British army!

"They'll fight if need be," Uncle Peter had said.

A few hours after the Braintree men marched away, Minutemen from the south streamed up the Shore Road. John Adams and his son greeted them all, offering food, water and rest beneath the elms. As night came on, the barn filled up, then the floor of the house, and latecomers had to pick their way through snoring bodies to find space enough to lie down.

All that night and the following day the men filed northward, while refugees from around Boston passed them moving south. They told an unbelievable story of the rout of eighteen hundred British regulars by an angry swarm of citizens. From behind stone walls and trees, the militiamen's deadly bullets had left a crimson trail of fallen Redcoats from Concord Bridge to Charlestown Neck.

Dissension had flamed into rebellion. There was no turning back. Campfires ringed Boston, sputtering defiance at the British Army. This time the Americans would not go home.

The excitement and confusion of those April days turned to lead in Johnny's heart as he watched the swelling procession of refugees fleeing down the Shore Road from Charlestown and occupied Boston. Abigail Adams offered them food and rest, but there was no solace for the homes and security left behind. Merchants and professional men with their household treasures stacked high in carriages seemed no less pitiful than laborers who carried their sparse belongings on their backs.

War was an ominous reality when John Adams set off against the stream of humanity toward Philadelphia for the second session of Congress. There were eight thousand British troops at Boston and residents up and down the coast lived in daily dread of invasion from the sea.

"Peter will watch out for you and the children," he told his wife as he bid them all a reluctant good-by.

Only a few weeks later, on a Sunday in May, Johnny was wakened at dawn by the clamor of church bells. His first thought was "They are coming," and he rushed barefoot to his garret window which faced toward the sea. A horde of people were hurrying up from the water front carrying or dragging an odd assortment of household goods, children, animals, even clothing. Uncle Peter was running among them toward the house, and Johnny tumbled down the steep staircase to the kitchen to meet him.

"Three British sloops and a cutter have dropped anchor below Great Hill," Peter told his brother's family. "They're launching longboats to bring the soldiers ashore. You'd best take the children and move inland, Abby, with the rest of the folks. Perhaps you can hide in the woods."

Abigail Adams refused to panic. "I'll not leave yet awhile, Peter," was her calm reply.

She sent Johnny up nearby Penn's Hill with his father's telescope, where he saw the longboats landing on tiny Grape Island just offshore. Hurrying back with the news, he found the militia already in the yard. His Uncle Elihu had just carried a pot from the kitchen, and the men gathered round to press molten liquid into their bullet molds. Johnny knew the militia lacked adequate ammunition, but what was this they were using?

Running to the kitchen he stared horrified at the wall above the hearth. All his mother's twinkling pewter spoons were gone! Behind him, his Uncle's gruff voice startled him.

"Well then, little soldier, what saw you from Penn's Hill?" Elihu put his arm around his nephew's shoulder, shaking him gently as he drew him back to the yard.

The Redcoats had only come to raid Grape Island for fodder for their horses and catch a few pigs that grazed there.

Mrs. Adams' pewter bullets drove them off. But a few weeks later, Johnny was again awakened before dawn, this time by a rumbling too persistent to be thunder. No sooner had the reverberations from one explosion rolled away to the west than another wave crashed down from Boston across the bay.

Down in the kitchen Johnny found his mother already shawled and clutching Papa's glass. Together they hurried up Penn's Hill, with Nabby and Charles close behind. That day they saw the smoke of the battle on Charlestown Neck, saw the flames that destroyed Charlestown, turning church steeples to pillars of fire. They could only imagine the anguish 'and the suffering.

The next afternoon, Sunday, June 18, Uncle Peter brought news of the defeat at Bunker and Breed's Hills, where the provincials had fought a magnificent defense to hold Charlestown Neck. He told of friends and neighbors dead on the ramparts.

Suddenly Peter noticed his nephew rubbing his fists against his eyes. "How they fought, Johnny!" he cried. "You'd have been proud!"

Johnny nodded understanding, but whatever pride he felt was swallowed up in a well of emptiness within him—an overwhelming feeling of loss, not only for the dead of Bunker Hill, but for the even tenor of his own life which he sensed could never be the same. His sister Nabby was weeping unashamedly, and the tears pressed against his own eyes and filled his throat. Without a word, he bolted up the stairs to his mother's room and hid himself in the depths of her closet, far back beneath the eaves. There the tears flowed unseen.

"Perhaps I should have waited till we were alone to tell the news, Abby?" Peter asked his sister-in-law.

Abigail Adams laid her hand fondly on her daughter's

head. "These children must learn to be adults before their childhood is half done," she told Peter. "I must try to make them understand the cause of the revolution is more important than the people involved. We must all make sacrifices."

In the troubled weeks that followed, Johnny sought the dark solace of his hideaway frequently. In July, George Washington was sent by the Congress to Cambridge to organize the provincial army. Many local militiamen joined him there—among them Johnny's beloved Uncle Elihu. In August the strapping vital man was dead of dysentery which was sweeping through the army. The new enemy rampaged down the coast, killing civilians as well as soldiers, old and young.

Within weeks, Grandmother Smith died of it at the parsonage in Weymouth, but Mrs. Adams had little time to mourn the loss of her mother. She herself was sick as were the children. Baby Tommy barely survived. Johnny watched the suffering, quietly helping as best he could, while the raw wound in his heart grew into a canker of hatred for those he believed caused it. Some of his feelings were reflected in letters to his father, whose comforting presence he missed more than ever.

"Johnny writes like a hero," John Adams wrote his wife. The boy's quick mind and ardent spirit, his passionate patriotism, almost frightened him.

Mrs. Adams respected the privacy of her son's hiding place until one day she smelled smoke in her bedroom. Candle in hand, she invaded his sanctum. The eight-year-old lad was huddled behind her dresses and chewing thoughtfully on his father's pipe. Gently she separated him from this new solace.

"You must learn to govern your emotions, Johnny," she told him. "Anger and resentment only disperse energy which should be used constructively."

To illustrate her words, she gave him a job to do. She had become impatient with the regular mail, which was uncertain and slow. Anxious for news from Congress, she decided to have Johnny ride "post" for her. Throughout the winter, he rode the eleven miles to Cambridge several times a week despite cold and drifting snow. The duty was a perfect outlet for the boy's frustrated energy, the camps at Cambridge a constant fascination.

Beneath the new United Colonies' flag, Johnny saw sharpshooters from the frontier in their buckskins, who appeared almost as wild as the Indians they were trained to fight. Beside them were encamped perfumed southern dandies, many of whom had brought their black body servants. The New England boy had never seen an African before. He liked their kind faces and soft accents and found himself wishing that his mother had a few to help her on the farm.

There were German folk from Pennsylvania whose guttural language mingled oddly with the staccato French dialect of volunteers from the disputed border country near Quebec. All these citizen soldiers were united in enthusiastic preparation of a surprise party for the British who sat snugly in Boston.

The Colonials had been unable to mount any sort of offensive to drive the enemy from the important port because they had no big guns and little powder. A Boston bookseller, Henry Knox, undertook to supply General Washington with the needed artillery. He brought the guns from captured British forts at Ticonderoga and Crown Point by sled across the snowy Berkshires. They were mounted atop Dorchester Heights behind bundles of hay and dirt that served as parapets, since the earth was too frozen to dig.

The British in Boston awoke one morning in March to the

throaty roar of big guns they never dreamed the Colonials had. The bombardment lasted three days and nights, and every rumble set Johnny's blood tingling as if he personally had lit the fuse. On Sunday, March 17, 1776, he stood on Penn's Hill cheering as all the British ships with their cargoes of Redcoats and Tory satellites sailed out of Boston Harbor.

In July, Abigail Adams took her children to Boston to be inoculated against smallpox. So it was that on Thursday, July 18, 1776, Johnny stood with his family in King Street. He had never seen the square in front of the Town House so crowded. People even stood on surrounding rooftops, and boys hung precariously from tree limbs.

On the balcony of the Town House, Tom Crafts, the house painter, dressed in the uniform of a colonel of the Continental Army, held a parchment aloft for all to see. Then he began to read: "The Unanimous Declaration of the Thirteen United States of America, in General Congress assembled."

The words of the Declaration of Independence drummed into Johnny's consciousness. Who could have dreamed such a brave dream—and put it into words!

". . . that all men are created equal . . . endowed by their Creator with certain unalienable Rights . . ."

"Well, my own papa for one," he heard himself say out loud.

Cannon boomed and bells rang. The crowd surged forward and tore the King's arms from the wall of the Town House. A shout went up and joy burst from Johnny's throat as his piping child's voice vowed a young man's dedication to the new nation.

"God bless the United States of America, and let all people say, Amen!"

★★★★★★★★★★★★★★★★★★★★★ **2** ★★★★★★★★★★★★★★★★★★★★★

Running the Blockade

Master Johnny maintained his footing on the deck of the frigate *Boston* by clinging to the rail. The ship seemed tiny as it sank in the trough between waves, shuddered as a comber hit her and boiled up over her freeboard, then staggered to the crest only to slide off the other side. Johnny swallowed hard to quiet his stomach, then squinted to glimpse the British man-of-war that had been chasing them for two days.

Beside him stood the reassuring figure of his father, conversing calmly with the ship's captain, Samuel Tucker. Near them was a chest containing all John Adams' papers, strapped and weighted, ready to be tossed overboard should the broad-beamed Britisher heave close enough for battle. Johnny knew that his father would follow it into the sea rather than risk capture, for John Adams was a traitor in British eyes, an instigator of rebellion, signer of the treasonous Declaration of Independence. This winter of 1778 he was sailing as special emissary from the Continental Congress to enlist France's aid against the motherland.

"Death in the sea would be better than being hanged," Johnny reminded himself severely, then began to shiver uncontrollably. His ten-year-old mind rejected either alternative. "They're falling back, sir," Captain Tucker told Mr. Adams. "I believe we've given them the slip. You and your young man should go below and get some rest."

Johnny crept into his stuffy little bunk and was asleep in moments. His father, writing at his table beneath the swaying lantern, noted thankfully that his son slept. He and Abigail had concurred that the trip, despite its dangers, was an experience young John should not miss. In Paris he could have formal schooling impossible in America with the schools disrupted by war. Old Ben Franklin had two grandsons studying at Passy, outside of Paris, and Silas Deane of Connecticut, one of the commissioners already in France, had asked John Adams to bring his son Jesse, too.

A mid-February blizzard had delayed their sailing for two days. When they finally nosed out of the Nantasket roadstead, gales and high seas had driven them back into Marblehead. Three days later they cleared Salem only to discover three British warships lying in wait for them off Cape Ann. They had played fox and geese across the wild Atlantic ever since. The father smiled fondly at the boy's peaceful expression and continued his letter to his wife.

"Johnny sends his duty to Mamma, and love to his sister and brothers. He behaves like a man!"

Johnny's rest was brief. The storm—which doubtless saved the *Boston* from capture—grew worse as they approached the Grand Banks. Lightning struck the mainmast with a crack that brought the sickest passengers topside, only to be ordered below again. Three sailors were knocked out while wind carried away the top of the cracked mast. Sails and rigging littered the decks. It was two days before they were cleared and the ship got fairly under way once more. Fortunately the sea was calmer and the only ship they sighted was a friendly Frenchman flying the colors of the Province of Normandy.

The weather continued calm though icy cold for two weeks. Johnny got his sea legs enough to enjoy life aboard ship. He and Jesse Deane investigated every nook and cranny of the privateer. The mate, Mr. Barrons, took the boys in tow, teaching them how to make complicated sailor's knots while he told them about his own family back in Massachusetts and spun endless yarns about his experiences at sea.

One morning in March the two boys were standing at the bow watching the blackfish jumping and blowing off their quarter, when Johnny's sharp eyes caught a blur of white on the horizon. At first he thought it was a gull.

"It might mean land is near," he told his companion gleefully, but the lookout's sharp cry from the crow's nest turned his joy to apprehension.

"Sail-ho!"

As the two ships sped toward each other across the choppy gray Atlantic, passengers and crew of the *Boston* gathered on the foredeck to see who the stranger might be. Johnny saw his father climbing up to the bridge and quietly followed. Captain Tucker was peering through his glass, and Johnny was just in time to hear him exclaim:

"T'is a nice fat merchantman, sir! I beg your leave to give chase. What a prize she would make!"

"Granted," Johnny heard his father's enthusiastic reply.

"Ho there," Captain Tucker shouted, "clear the decks! Prepare the guns, Mr. Barrons."

The Britisher altered course to avoid them but the *Boston* gave chase. It was nearly 3:00 P.M. before they came up on their quarry.

"Put a shot across her bows, Mr. Barrons," the captain ordered.

There was a flash, an explosion, an agonizing shriek from the deck below. Flame licked across the deck from the twisted gun, and Johnny realized it had blown out its breech. The mate had been thrown clear across the deck where he lay against the bulwark like a discarded rag doll. Johnny noted sickly that blood was oozing out of one leg. He started to go to his friend but his father motioned him back, then dashed down the ladder toward the injured man.

The Britisher returned their fire, carrying away the mizzen yard. The loosened sail cracked in the wind like a musket, but Captain Tucker's roar was louder.

"Give 'em another gun, damn it!"

The merchantmen replied surprisingly to the American's second shot by striking her colors. Captain Tucker was preparing to send a boarding party to her when Johnny remembered Mr. Barrons. He found his father coming out of the mate's cabin, looking more grim and shaken than Johnny ever recalled seeing him.

"The leg had to be amputated," Mr. Adams told his son.

"Mr. Barrons said the guns were no good," Johnny said angrily. The father only shook his head sadly.

News of the capture cheered them. The ship *Martha* out of London was a fat prize indeed, with a cargo insured by Lloyds for £70,000.

"Best of all, 'tis supplies for the British troops in New York," Captain Tucker told Minister Adams gleefully. "Now we'll send her with a prize crew into Boston where they surely need that cargo more!"

There was a joyous bustle as the passengers prepared letters to send home with the *Martha*, but Johnny could not get Mr.

Barrons off his mind. He and Jesse hovered near his door all the next week. The snow-topped mountains of Spain were gleaming on the horizon when the big man died, and they buried him in the sea he had loved.

The voyage became a nightmare memory supplanted by a strange lovely dream as the ship ran north and east along the coast which dipped away from the craggy white-crested Pyrenees to France's green meadows rimmed with sand.

On Saturday, March 28, six weeks after leaving Massachusetts Bay, the *Boston* sailed into the crowded roadstead at the mouth of the Gironde River. Johnny and Jesse excitedly watched the ships from many lands that passed to and fro or rode quietly at anchor. At Pauillac, a swarthy pilot boarded the *Boston*, and skillfully guided the ship up the river, until, early Tuesday morning, Johnny saw the city of Bordeaux off their bow, rose-tinted in the dawn. The low buildings were of light-colored plaster or stone that glowed when the light struck them. He thought them vastly more beautiful than the wooden shacks which sprawled down to the shore at Boston.

On closer acquaintance the French port proved noisy, its streets narrow and smelly. The Americans were not tempted to linger, but took a stage immediately for Paris. The lush countryside was dotted with clusters of bright-roofed peasant cottages and punctuated by manor houses half-hidden behind avenues of poplars—a fairyland to a boy who had never traveled farther than Boston.

The party went directly to the home of Benjamin Franklin in Passy, near the Bois de Boulogne, where Jesse Deane was reunited with his father. The boys were already enrolled in school with Franklin's two grandsons, William Temple Franklin and Benjamin Franklin Bache. Besides the usual studies, their master, Monsieur Le Coeur, instructed them in the fine arts of fencing, dancing, music and drawing—niceties unheard of in the average New England school.

Johnny was an enthusiastic French student. Monsieur Le Coeur had his boys practice by acting in simple plays produced by a company of children in the Bois de Boulogne. The dramatic arts were frowned on by many in puritan New England, but at the Théâtre des Petits Comédiens Johnny developed a passion for the stage.

Each Sunday the American boys attended high mass at the nearby Church of the Minimes, a lengthy ceremony that meant nothing to them. Johnny's Congregational grandfather, William Smith, had implanted in him a deep faith in God and in the Christian precepts. Every night of his life he knelt beside his bed to say his prayers.

"But all that pomp and ritual just doesn't seem right," he complained to his father. John Adams was curiously unsympathetic.

"You must say nothing against the religion as long as you are in this country. If you are to be a statesman or a diplomat, you must learn to respect—and try to understand—all men's beliefs and customs."

John Adams did abet his son in a campaign for more free days on which to tour Paris and the surrounding countryside. The treaties of alliance and commerce he had come to negotiate had been signed before his arrival. Now he was determined to make good use of the time until new orders came. He showed Johnny the Palace at Versailles, the Military School in Paris, the Cathedral of Notre Dame where they laughed delightedly at the ugly gargoyles that guarded the towers.

They rode in the donkey carts at the Jardin des Plantes and went to the zoo—and neither father nor son would admit to the other the homesickness that grew to a nagging ache as the months went by.

"I envy you," Johnny wrote Charles, "the pleasure of being where you can look upon the rugged rocks and homely pasture . . . and converse with our Mamma, sister and brother. Such pleasures are not exceeded by all the gaiety and riches of Europe. For myself, I am convinced that your opportunities are as good as mine, despite all the difficulties and dangers I have gone through. But," he concluded bravely, "we are sent into this world for some end, and it is our duty to discover it, then pursue it with unconquerable perseverance."

Johnny wrung every possible benefit from his experiences in France. His father was delighted with his progress at school, his discreet conduct in company and especially his rapid mastery of the language. He urged his son to keep a diary, but Johnny balked at this new task. He wrote his mother that he would be mortified a few years hence to read his childish nonsense.

"A journal book of a lad of eleven years of age," he rationalized, "cannot be expected to contain much of science, literature, arts, wisdom or wit."

But his mother could tell by his letters how his mind was growing. By September he was writing principally in French.

Christmas in France was a particular wonder to Johnny. This year, the brilliance of the fête was enhanced by the birth of the Princess Maria Theresa Charlotte, Fille du Roi. Johnny and his father walked from their lodgings at Passy into Paris to see the illumination in honor of the new princess. All the public buildings, the schools and palaces and hospitals, were splendid in candlelit garlands.

"But the expense, Papa!" gasped the New England lad,

"at least a million livres!" Young as he was, Johnny had noted the poverty of the workers and peasants as compared to the opulence of the nobles and the court. His stanch republican sensibilities were offended.

The illumination was one of Johnny's last outings. In March his father determined to go home since no new orders, and no funds, had arrived from Congress. Indeed little news came from the farm at Braintree. Those of Mrs. Adams' letters that did get past the Royal Navy's tight blockade brought disturbing news of hardship and food shortages. Most farm hands were off fighting the war. Prices of even necessities like straight pins had soared out of reason. But worst of all was the undercurrent of loneliness.

Johnny and his father left Paris in March, but it was May before they found a ship from the port of Nantes to take them home.

The reunion in Braintree was sweet but achingly brief. In August, 1779, a few weeks after their return, John Adams was dispatched again to Europe as Minister Plenipotentiary to handle negotiations for peace with Britain. He decided to take Charles, now nine, and his tutor, Cousin Thaxter. Johnny did not want to go again. He had his heart set on entering Andover Academy to prepare for Harvard and a career in law. His father appeared satisfied with his decision, but one Sunday evening after church his mother drew him aside.

"In human probability," she told him, "it will do more for your education to go back to France than to prepare for college at Andover."

"But Father complains now that my education is retarded!" Johnny argued.

His mother stood in troubled silence beside the hearth. The firelight seemed to accentuate the lines of fatigue and worry that had appeared on her pretty face since last Johnny saw her, and lit each new strand of silver in her smooth brown hair.

"When first you accompanied your father to Europe," she answered quietly, "it was difficult to bring my mind to part with a child so young. But you have already gained knowledge far beyond the average boy of your age. Now you are older, you should benefit even more from your experiences. I believe God has placed unusual talents in your hands, of which an account will be demanded of you hereafter. . . ."

Abigail Adams looked fondly at her twelve-year-old son, now grown as tall as herself. "You know I would rather have you here with me."

On November 13, Johnny was back asea in a cabin of the *La Sensible.* That evening he began the diary that his father had been urging him to keep.

The reluctance Johnny had felt about this second voyage was soon dissipated by his natural curiosity. The day after they sailed he knew every passenger aboard and most of the crew. In addition to his brother Charles, two other boys his age were being sent to Europe in his father's care. Their presence enlivened the voyage, and Johnny felt very superior when gales sent them to their bunks while he was still on his feet.

Two weeks out, the guns were lashed down because of the roll. He took his turn at the pumps with the other able-bodied passengers, working in round-the-clock shifts. The pumpers soon realized that the water in the hold was gaining on them despite their efforts. They appointed Master John, the only French linguist among them, to demand an explanation of the captain, Chevalier Bidé de Chavagnes.

"There is a hole in our bottom as large as a man's head,"

the captain admitted, "but do not tell the others as it might upset them. We must put into Spain with all speed!"

This information unnerved Johnny somewhat since he felt they could not make port in less than three weeks. But Captain de Chavagnes had no appetite for a cold Atlantic grave. He crowded on sail and made a beeline for Spain. On December 8, *La Sensible* rode quietly at anchor in the bowl-like harbor of El Ferrol, having made a record crossing of less than four weeks.

The snow-topped Pyrenees above their anchorage offered a new challenge when the captain assured his passengers that the ship could not be made seaworthy for at least a month. Minister Adams determined to continue the journey overland, though there was no regular post, nor were any horses available. Once into the mountains, they realized that only the mules they finally obtained could have clambered over the steep paths anyway.

The long journey over the mountains in midwinter had no ill effect on the sturdy boys except for colds. Johnny got a new view of Europe that was disillusioning. Lodgings in the mountain villages—public and private—were filthy. Peasants' cottages consisted of one room, smoke-filled since there was no chimney. Man and beast huddled around a fire built on the dirt floor beneath a hole cut into the roof.

To offset the discomfort and boredom of the trip, Thaxter set the boys to learning Spanish. For want of anything to write, Johnny filled the pages of his new diary with sketches of warships, which he named *H.M.S. Frightful* and *H.M.S. Horrid,* and forts, cannon and soldiers on parade.

Arrival at M. Le Coeur's school at Passy in February was a homecoming for Johnny, but he had only a few months to enjoy the company of his old schoolmates. Minister Adams was sent to the Netherlands to negotiate loans for his penniless government. He put the boys in the public Latin School in Amsterdam in September, and in January, 1781, Johnny, now thirteen years old, matriculated at the University of Leyden, the most celebrated university in all Europe.

He lodged with Benjamin Waterhouse, a Bostonian taking advanced medical studies. The older student showed Johnny around the ancient town and introduced him to the mysteries of university life. They rented horses on week ends or after classes and galloped across the barren gray countryside where only the long-armed windmills marked the distances. Johnny experienced the breathless exhilaration of skating on Holland's endless canals. But the carefree days were brief. In March, his father paid a visit to his lodgings.

"Charles is so homesick now that you are not with him," he told Johnny, "that I must have Cousin Thaxter take him home."

"He's younger than I was when we first came," Johnny reminded his father, "and I was fearfully homesick."

"You never told me." John Adams shook his head. "Well— you are content now?"

"Oh yes . . ." Johnny started to describe his new-found pleasures, but his father stopped him.

"A grand new opportunity has come to you, Johnny. One that I feel—and I know your mother would agree—you should seize."

Johnny felt himself go tense with apprehension. His father hurried on.

"Our good friend, Francis Dana, is being sent by Congress as minister to St. Petersburg. He will try to gain recognition for the United States and negotiate treaties of alliance and commerce with the Empress Catherine. He needs a secretary who speaks and writes French. He asked especially for you, Johnny."

Johnny went through agony that night, seeing all his plans evaporate. Why could he never be allowed to lead a normal life? Must he always be different? Yet even as he ranted against his fate, he knew he would go. The journey to Russia as the minister's secretary offered more education and experience than any university. The words of one of his mother's recent letters rang in his mind like the muster bell.

"Great necessities call out great virtues."

Across the Atlantic in his native land, men were fighting and dying that a nation might live. No life maintained a measured beat. He, too, had certain obligations.

Apprentice Diplomat

A few days after John Quincy's fourteenth birthday, he left Amsterdam on a strange odyssey across middle Europe into the mysterious realm of the Muscovites. Few Americans ever made this trip into the heart of Europe. He felt like a modern Marco Polo as he and Francis Dana journeyed across Germany to Berlin, thence north along the coast of the Baltic Sea to Danzig, Konigsberg and Riga before swinging inland to St. Petersburg.

The German countryside he thought neat and pretty, much like Holland. In Berlin, peasant cottages were interspersed with handsome new buildings. The travelers learned that Frederick II, King of Prussia, intended to replace all the people's dark little dwellings with large modern apartments. John Quincy thought it a very enlightened thing to do, but he noticed the people themselves did not seem too happy about the change.

"Perhaps that is because they have no choice in the matter," Mr. Dana surmised.

As they traveled on through Germany, they discovered that the people had little choice about anything. Every able-bodied male must serve in the King's Army—except the eldest son of each family who was tied to the land on which he was born. The fruits of all his labor went to the noble who owned his tiny tract, and if it was sold, he and his family were sold with it.

"Why they're no better off than the slaves on the plantations in America!" John Quincy exclaimed.

"And this feudal system still exists over most of Europe," reminded his companion.

John Quincy was beginning to realize how radical was the Declaration of Independence. In Russia, for the first time in his life, he saw human beings bought and sold like cattle.

"No wonder father was determined that slavery be abolished in Massachusett's new constitution," he mused. "And it should be outlawed throughout the United States!"

"That may be your battle, Master John," Dana laughed. "We've not even won independence for ourselves yet."

The Russian capital, St. Petersburg, was like no city the Americans had ever seen. Even at a distance, in the haze of the late August sunset, it looked different. Suddenly John Quincy realized why. Squat domes replaced the church spires that marked every western city. The public buildings and palaces had an oriental splendor. John Quincy almost forgot the squalor of the countryside, even overlooked the malodorous back streets of the capital itself, as he was swept into the vortex of a society more glittering than that which surrounded His Most Christian Majesty Louis XVI.

As interpreter for Mr. Dana, he attended all official functions. The other diplomats, the Russian nobles, even the doughty old Empress herself—all were charmed by the handsome golden-haired youth who behaved with poise worthy of a nobleman. The ladies of the court were bold in their attentions to the young American, awakening in him an appreciation of their charms that he found quite alarming.

"I am constantly exposed to moral dangers," he wrote a friend, "and only through the mercy of Providence do I not succumb."

He did succumb to the banquets and balls where M. Le Coeur's dancing lessons served him well. He thrilled to the incomparable ballet, the concerts and the plays.

"But I do feel guilty," he told Minister Dana, "when I remember that all the luxury and opulence of the court society rests on a perfect mountain of human misery."

"Old Catherine is a tyrant," Dana conceded, "and every noble commands an army of serfs. But we are not here to convert them," warned the senior diplomat.

When not performing his secretarial duties, John Quincy applied himself to his studies. He was determined not to fall behind, though no schools or teachers were available except, he wrote his father, at a cost "very dear." He elaborated:

"There is nobody here but slaves and princes. The slaves can't have their children instructed, the nobility send theirs abroad. There is not even a library for public use in the city, only the English library to which Mr. Dana subscribes."

He devoured several historical works, then rewarded himself with Voltaire and the English poets. He translated Cicero's orations. A smattering of German and Russian were added to his lengthening list of languages. Russian history and customs he studied in detail. In addition, he made the reading of a chapter of the Bible a daily habit, as his father and mother had always done.

The frozen countryside prohibited travel during the winter, but John Quincy took advantage of the warmer days to explore the city. When spring came, he and Mr. Dana drove often into the country. The grinding poverty on the farms and in the towns was very apparent. Often when they stopped at the lavish country estate of a friend, the young American was tempted to tax his host with the condition of his serfs. Mr. Dana always forestalled him with a warning glance. He must not prejudice their mission.

Though their reception was hospitable, it soon became apparent that their mission was fruitless. Catherine had no intention of risking Britain's wrath by recognizing her rebellious colonies as a nation.

Meanwhile, across the sea, the war for that savage land was swinging to the advantage of the Americans and their French allies. In October, a major victory was won at Yorktown, and in the spring of 1782, John Adams wrote from The Hague that he hoped for early peace. The Dutch had already signed a treaty of recognition and alliance and had promised the United States ambassador the much-needed loan.

"It will be well if you prepare to join me as soon as possible," he wrote his son, "so that we may start for home immediately after negotiations are concluded."

The boy was as eager as his father to go home after three years' absence. Francis Dana, however, continued to work for Russia's recognition. So John Quincy waited through the best traveling months until, in September, his father wrote that negotiations at The Hague were completed, and the first permanent legation in Europe was established—L'Hôtel des Etats-Unis.

"I shall sign the Treaty of Commerce next week," John Adams exulted. "The standard of the United States waves at The Hague in triumph—over insolence and British pride."

John Quincy could delay no longer. On October 30, he and Count Greco, a secretary of the Italian embassy, started

for Sweden in the face of the lowering Arctic winter. They
were delayed, sometimes for weeks, by storms, bad roads and
frozen water passages, but were armed with letters of introduction from friends in St. Petersburg that insured them a
hospitable reception everywhere. The New England lad was
welcomed in the homes of leading merchants and government
officials in Sweden, Norway and Denmark. He danced with
their daughters, visited the museums, attended concerts and
the theater.

As a junior ambassador of good will without portfolio, he
found opportunity for serious diplomatic work, too. Swedish
businessmen were anxious to trade with the United States.

"No one ever doubted independence would be won," they
assured him. "Already a minister to the United States has been
named."

Mention of the new country was always a signal for a
toast. Then John Quincy would assure his hosts that his country would welcome a commercial exchange. The fifteen-year-
old boy found himself advising seasoned merchants in
Norrköping, Stockholm, Goteborg and Copenhagen as to
the best exports for America.

". . . but send the list to be checked by our emissary at St.
Petersburg, Mr. Francis Dana," the wise neophyte urged.

From Copenhagen, by land and sea to Hamburg in northern
Prussia, was no more than three hundred English miles, but
it took the travelers a month. John Quincy began to feel a
sense of urgency to reach his father, but at Hamburg they
were detained for another month until April turned the key
of their winter prison.

On April 20, 1783, six months after leaving St. Petersburg,
John Quincy finally arrived at The Hague, only to find his
father was in Paris. The boy's disappointment was offset by

the news that a treaty of peace and independence had been in effect since January. The United States—his United States —was truly born.

Hope of an early return home eluded the Adams men again, since details of the peace remained to be worked out with a British delegation in Paris. But their own reunion was some compensation. The plump little father beamed approvingly at his erect young son. Little trace of the awkward schoolboy remained. Downy fluff softened the sharp line of his finely molded jaw. His chiseled nose and arched brows gave him an arrogant look, but humor lurked in his intelligent blue eyes, and turned the corners of his mouth engagingly upward.

"You've arrived just in time," John Adams told his son. "The peace commission can certainly use an experienced secretary like yourself."

Dr. Franklin was living in the same house in Passy. At seventy-eight, the remarkable man was as busy as ever. Philosophers and politicians, diplomats and princes strolled through his drawing room as casually as neighbors strolled through Abigail Adams' kitchen in Braintree.

John Quincy's life in Paris was very different from his student days. With his father, Dr. Franklin and John Jay, the famous New York lawyer who was the third peace commissioner, he attended all the conference sessions. Diplomatic sparring fascinated him as a wrestling match might thrill another man. In spidery script, he transcribed several of the historic peace documents, which were signed at Versailles on September 3, 1783.

Outside the conference chamber was a gaudy dream life in which the plain farmer-lawyer from Massachusetts and his son were frequent visitors at the glittering court of His Most Christian Majesty and his lovely queen, Marie Antoinette. It was a life filled with painted bejeweled ladies in towering powdered headdresses squired by men in satin breeches and pointed red-heeled slippers. John Quincy thought them absurd, but he was glad he had saved the money Mr. Dana had paid him. At sixteen he was anxious to participate in all the pleasures Paris offered. He purchased velvet breeches, a silken coat and long silk hose, and he learned to powder his hair. A young man must be properly attired!

He and his father dined often with the Marquis de Lafayette and his lady. Their home was a refreshing change from the extravagances of the court. John Quincy had met Madame la Marquise as a boy and felt at home with her. Her kind face had never known powder or paint, any more than had his mother's.

Lafayette, who had fought in America's war for independence, spoke ominously of the rumblings beneath Paris' gay exterior. "Voyez-vous, mes amis, such inequities cannot continue! My country is near bankruptcy. Louis tries to correct some evils, but his frivolous queen! She is extravagant, like a child! The nobles that surround them are utterly blind and selfish." Lafayette raised his hands in a gesture of helplessness. "Poor Louis is misled and blocked at every turn."

With the peace concluded, John Quincy thought he should return to America to get on with his studies, but his father persuaded him to linger.

"There is still the commercial treaty to be drawn up," he reminded the apprentice diplomat. "Tom Jefferson will be here soon to work on it, and it's an education just to know him. Your mother speaks of joining us in the spring with Nabby."

Father and son traveled to London together to meet the

ladies. When their ship was delayed, John Adams returned to Paris. Alone in London, John Quincy walked all over the old city. The narrow streets had dingy brick houses and the banks of the Thames were disfigured with dirty old stables and warehouses.

The museums and libraries, the lectures at the Royal Institution off Piccadilly, the presentations at the Opera House in Haymarket Street, made up for the lack of beauty of the capital itself. In Parliament, he listened enthralled to William Pitt, the Prime Minister, and the masterly parliamentarian, Lord North, whose very name had once struck terror to the heart of every good American.

On the eve of John Quincy's seventeenth birthday, his mother and sister arrived unexpectedly at the Hotel Osborne where he lodged. After five years' separation they seemed like two strangers. Nabby, his childhood playmate, was a vivacious dark-eyed beauty of nineteen, while his mother—he didn't remember her being so small!

"Oh Johnny, you've grown so tall," Mrs. Adams cried, and he laughed. His mother stared and stared—for the forlorn little boy who had left her so unwillingly was an exquisite man of the world with handsome silk-clad calves beneath velvet knee-breeches, and immaculate stock and linen trimmed with real lace.

John Adams had rented a gracious white house in Auteuil outside Paris. Surrounded by a small, tree-shaded park, it had a secluded garden where Abigail could feel at home. Certainly everything else was strange to the New England woman. John Quincy squired her and Nabby around Paris. He showed them the Tuilleries with its gardens and statues and Notre Dame with its grinning gargoyles. They drove on the Champs

Élysées, in the Bois de Boulogne and out to see the Palace at Versailles.

"The palaces are magnificent," Mrs. Adams admitted, "but big and cold to live in!"

"The Queen's bathing room is as big as our parlor," John Quincy assured her. "They say it's all marble with gold fittings."

He took them to the fête at Longchamps where splendid carriages paraded.

"It is 'de rigueur'—a must—to come to the fête," John Quincy told them, "to see and be seen."

✦ "The men are as powdered and painted as their ladies," Nabby exclaimed. "One can't tell what they look like. They might be puppets."

"Oh look!" Mrs. Adams clapped a gloved hand to her mouth. "Can that be William Temple, Dr. Franklin's grandson?" she whispered. "Why he's leading a cat on a ribbon!"

They went often to tea with Dr. Franklin and with Madame de Lafayette. When lanky, red-headed Tom Jefferson arrived in Paris for the commercial negotiations with Britain, he became their frequent companion at the theater and opera.

"I love to be with Mr. Jefferson," John Quincy told his father.

"You will never meet a man of more universal learning," the elder Adams conceded.

John Quincy knew he should think about going home. If he was ever to amount to anything he must go to Harvard and get his law degree. He was anxious to see Charles, who would be entering the university in the fall, and young Thomas. It was hard to think of that toddler as a sprout going into his teens! But after seven years of travel, the prospect of being subjected to the rules of a college and the tedious study of law was not particularly tantalizing.

In April, 1785, his father was appointed by Congress to be the first American minister to the Court of St. James. John Quincy confessed to his mother that the thought of a winter in London was tempting.

"And I should love to have you with me there," she told him. "I fear I shall cut an awkward figure at court. But," she went on seriously, "your father has been so taken up with public interests that his own fortune has suffered. His children must learn to provide for themselves."

"Well, I shall never be able to do so if I linger in Europe much longer," John Quincy admitted. "I must say, their system has made me a confirmed republican. Only in America have I hope of living independent and free, and I'd rather die than live otherwise."

★★★★★★★★★★★★★★★★★★★★★★★   ★★★★★★★★★★★★★★★★★★★★★★★

4

"Forget the Patriot's Theme!"

At dawn on Sunday, July 17, 1785, John Quincy stood on the bridge of the French packet *Captain Le Fournier*, staring at the tantalizing shores of his homeland. The captain had dropped anchor just outside the narrow passage between Long Island and Staten Island and refused to go further.

He stood on one side of John Quincy pouring out a torrent of excited French, while on the other side, an exasperated pilot tried to make him understand his directions. Between them, John Quincy labored to translate the English sea terms that were strange to him into French sea terms he knew no better.

"The pilot says that the channel is easy to follow," he assured the captain. "I will translate his directions literally. The worst thing one can strike is a sand bar—which could do your sturdy ship little harm." As the captain started to remonstrate, he added firmly, "We cannot remain anchored here forever!"

Soothed by the composure of his youthful passenger, the

captain decided to risk the strange waters. By noon, John Quincy was bouncing over the cobbled streets of the port of New York in a hansom cab. He found the low wooden buildings near the docks no more esthetically pleasing than those in London. Much had not been rebuilt after the great fire following the British occupation. But in Wall Street, trees shaded dignified mansions, and as they approached the Hudson River, he saw the City Hall with its colonnaded balcony standing neat and proud.

John Quincy stopped ten days with his father's old friend Richard Henry Lee, now president of Congress, to whom he delivered documents and letters from the commission in Paris. Then by packet and stage he returned to Massachusetts for a reunion with his brothers.

John Quincy did not know how lonely he had been for them until he saw the two big boys—now almost men—approaching down the wharf. They had missed all their youth together, and now were strangers.

"We'll make up for lost time when you come to Harvard," Charles told him. Charles was to enter the university that fall, while Thomas was preparing at the Latin School. Now they must separate again, for Charles and Thomas were staying in Braintree with Mrs. Adams' sister Mary, and her husband Richard Cranch, while John Quincy was to go to another sister, Betsy, in Haverhill. Her husband, the Reverend John Shaw, would tutor him in mathematics, Greek and Latin for the entrance examinations.

"Study hard so we'll be together sooner," the boys admonished their new-found brother.

John Quincy did. In six months he mastered material that ordinarily required two years to cover. In April, 1786, he was examined by President Willard, three professors and four tutors and was admitted to the junior class at Harvard. Dr. Benjamin Waterhouse, with whom he had lodged at Leyden and who was now a professor of medicine, told him that the professors had been astonished at the extent of his knowledge.

". . . especially since you pursued your studies without help, for the most part. But," his old friend warned, "be on guard against any air of superiority amongst the students."

"I thought I did poorly at the examination," the new student confessed. "I was very nervous and stammered over the Latin which I find difficult to speak."

Because of his father's service to his country, John Quincy was charged no tuition and he was allowed to live at the college, in Hollis Hall. Charles proudly introduced his brother to a number of "amiable and respectable characters." He became one of a merry group who gathered around a cider jug of an evening in the room of one or another to debate good-naturedly or practice on their musical instruments. John Quincy became an accomplished flute player, though his voice was admittedly no asset to any chorus.

"I have never before enjoyed the company of young men of my own age and disposition," he told Charles as they rode toward Quincy for their Christmas holiday. "I have never worked harder, nor ever been happier."

"Don't you miss the gay European social life?" asked Charles.

"Not at all!" was the answer. "My only regret is that I did not enter college two years ago. Though I must admit the experience has reduced my opinion of myself," he added laughing.

John Quincy was graduated from Harvard University with honors, Phi Beta Kappa, on July 16, 1787. He was chosen to make the commencement address, which was considered so outstanding that it was reprinted in Philadelphia's famous *Columbian Centinel*. The *Massachusetts Centinel* thought the ambassador's son "showed himself to be warmly attached to the republican system."

"Anyone who has lived in Europe would be," was his dry comment. He was surprised at the attention, since public speaking was difficult for him, and he could not keep his voice from squeaking and cracking.

Finding a lawyer with whom to serve his apprenticeship was his chief concern. His father wrote from London recommending Theophilus Parsons of Newburyport, ". . . since I am not at leisure to instruct you myself," he added regretfully.

John Quincy traveled to the picturesque North Shore seaport that September, resolved to devote himself entirely to the study of law. He took lodgings in State Street near Attorney Parson's office.

Newburyport was not, however, the quiet town he imagined. Three exuberant young men were also reading law with the distinguished Theophilus. Lawyer Parsons himself was one of the most stimulating men John Quincy had ever been associated with. He would settle in an old rocking chair after hours, cut off a quid of tobacco, and, fixing his students with penetrating eyes that shone beneath his jutting black brows, discourse on literature, philosophy or science as often as on the law.

"I believe he is as widely read as Mr. Jefferson or Dr. Franklin—or even my father!" John Quincy told his fellow students.

Politics was a frequent topic of discussion. A new constitution was being drawn up in convention at Philadelphia, where George Washington presided over a distinguished group from every state. Many had been signers of the Declaration. Even eighty-one-year-old Franklin, home finally from France, sat with them. Most were strong-government men who wished to weld the loose confederation of American states into a closer union. Not all considered the change desirable. Men like Thomas Jefferson and Patrick Henry were conspicuously absent from the constitutional convention.

Lawyer Parsons' fledglings argued every step as if theirs was the decision. Often they retired to Sawyer's Tavern to continue the discussion over beer mugs or big-bellied wine bottles. One evening they found a group of local young people partying there and were invited to join the dancing. The young men were drawn into a gay round of dances, dinners, sleigh rides and taffy pulls.

John Quincy and his flute were in great demand when the men walked out to serenade the ladies. He discovered the art of making love on a speeding sleigh with the thermometer at zero. Snuggled in furs and rugs beneath a winter's moon, the pastime, he decided, was one of the better Yankee inventions, worthy of a poet's descriptive powers. His law books gathered dust as he worked over romantic verses dedicated to a succession of saucy hoop-skirted ladies with scented beribboned curls.

He met Mary Frazier in January, and the other girls faded into the background. She was his constant companion on picnics and boat rides that spring. Her blond beauty, her wit and grace enthralled him—and worried him. He confided in his "second father," Francis Dana, now a justice of the Massachusetts Supreme Court, whom he always visited when in Cambridge.

"Happiness in life, I am fully persuaded, is derived principally from domestic attachments," John Quincy declared, after telling his old friend of his infatuation with Mary.

"But you are a penniless student," warned Judge Dana. His young friend's face showed the strain of controlling the passionate nature he usually hid so well.

"I must try not to be with her so much." John Quincy flung himself out of his chair and began pacing the judge's chamber. "Now about that case we just heard. . . ."

That summer, the elder Adamses returned from London. John Quincy and his brothers met them in Boston and returned to vacation with them in Braintree. Only Nabby was missing from the reunion. During her six years abroad, glowing letters to her brothers described her impressions, her social life, and finally, her growing attachment for the Secretary of Legation William Smith, to whom she was now married. With their two young sons, the Smiths had remained to transfer the legation to John Adams' successor.

John Adams had purchased the Vassal Mansion in Braintree some time ago. Now, in its spacious rooms, the Adamses received an unending stream of callers—neighbors and friends who came to welcome them after their long absence. There were teas and dinners and clambakes on the beach. The boys swam in Quincy's Creek and practiced together on violins and flute. When John Quincy returned to Newburyport in September, he had fallen far behind in his studies. He became so nervous trying to make up the lost time that he developed insomnia.

So he was home again in October, tramping the fields with his gun or riding his horse across hills bright with autumn leaves. He was there for the town's mammoth celebration when his father was chosen by representatives of the thirteen states to serve as George Washington's Vice-President under the new federal Constitution. He thought he would burst with pride when he saw his parents smiling and waving from their festooned coach as they drove off toward New York —seat of the new government. Hordes of cheering neighbors sped them on their way.

"No couple is more deserving of such an honor," John Quincy told his Aunt Mary, who stood beside him on the mansion steps.

With all the excitement and his earnest efforts to forget her, Mary Frazier's blue eyes held the same enchantment when he returned again to Newburyport.

"All my hopes of future happiness center in possession of that girl," he confided to his friends. "She becomes more and more a menace to my peace of mind. I must declare my love and throw myself on her mercy!"

On a spring evening while they sat in Mary's garden he whispered of his love. The eighteen-year-old girl listened quietly, then turned her lovely face to his and smiled. Suddenly he held her close.

"Wait, Johnny, wait! We must speak to father!" She broke away and ran toward the house.

Selectman Moses Frazier was in no hurry to marry off his eldest daughter, even to the son of the Vice-President.

"You are without profession, nor even very good prospects," he explained kindly. "Come back when you've made a place for yourself."

John Quincy knew Moses Frazier was right. He could not tie Mary down with promises.

"You will find someone worthier than I," he assured her.

"I do not believe such a man exists," she told him, making his decision to leave her free doubly difficult.

That September, John Quincy visited his family in the Vice-President's home on Richmond Hill, overlooking the Hudson River and the wheat fields beyond. He went with his father to Federal Hall—the same City Hall he had admired on his return from Europe—where George Washington presided over the new government of the United States. He had not seen the idol of his boyhood since the days when he rode post to Cambridge. The burdens and anguish of the war years were etched deeply in the great man's handsome face. But his kindly interest and ready humor had not changed.

When John Quincy told his mother about Mary, she shook her head sympathetically. "President Washington remarked how tired you look," she told her son. "But he had heard you were more attentive to your books than to the ladies. For once the President was misinformed!"

At Richmond Hill, he was reunited with Nabby, and introduced to her husband and his two small nephews, William Steuben and John Adams Smith. Playing with them and relaxing with his family, the insomnia that had begun to plague him again vanished, and he returned to his studies refreshed.

On July 15, 1790, John Quincy stood for the bar examination and was formally admitted to practice law in the courts of Essex County, Massachusetts. In the second week of August, after a month's vacation in Braintree, he packed up his father's law books and moved into a tiny office in Court Street, Boston, in a house owned by his father. At twenty-three he owned nothing, nor did clients immediately beat a path to his door.

Sitting in a musty office did not suit his impatient nature. Judge Dana threw some cases his way, but they were small civil suits that only made him more gloomy about the future. When he had to appear in court, he became agitated and self-conscious.

"I have no talent for extemporary speechifying," he wrote his mother. "Judge for yourself the figure I make in court!"

Many of his Harvard classmates were getting started in business or one of the professions. With Nathan Frazier, Mary's brother, and Daniel Sargent, also from Newburyport, the young men formed a group they named the Crackbrain Club. It was intended to be an intellectual discussion group, as the name implied, but John Quincy thought the taverns where they met were more conducive to gaiety than to sober reflection. They did interest themselves in local politics and attended town meetings. John Quincy was intrigued with governmental problems. He served on a number of committees, including one to reform the Boston police, but fast-moving events on the international scene soon commanded his attention.

Lafayette and the moderate republicans of France had succeeded in setting up a constitutional monarchy in 1790, but it lasted less than a year. Revolutionaries seized the government, imprisoning Louis and Marie Antoinette with all their court. No one with noble blood, no one suspected of serving or sympathizing with the erstwhile rulers, escaped the people's vengeance. Even Lafayette was branded a traitor when he attempted to save the king and queen from humiliation at the hands of the mob. He was hounded into exile with other moderates, while the radical Robespierre ushered in the reign of the guillotine.

When first the people of France proclaimed a republic, the American public hailed it warmly. Jacobin Clubs were formed, people took to calling each other "citizen" and "citizeness," simplified their dress, and a few men even cut their hair to appear more "republican." When some members of the Crackbrain Club affected such mannerisms, they were received with good-natured laughter. Arguments over existing forms of government were in the same lighthearted vein.

"Every throne in Europe is become a precarious perch," cried Tommy Crafts, son of the housepainter-colonel whom John Quincy had heard read America's Declaration of Independence. The young republican raised his glass for a toast:

"Let them topple like ninepins!"

John Quincy took a more serious view of the trend in France. Reports of the mounting terror were, for him, a personal nightmare. He would not join the toast.

"Awake or asleep, I seem to see my friends being marched to their death," he said.

"But they were dissolute, selfish and vain," Tommy argued. "They allowed the people to live like pigs while they wallowed in luxury. You have told us so yourself."

John Quincy tried to recall the bejeweled painted figures with their high red heels and towering powdered headdresses.

"They were like puppets," he mused, recalling Nabby's description. "I do not believe half of them knew how their countrymen lived. The thought of all those proud heads bent to that grisly chopping block is horrifying!"

Few Americans could reconcile liberty with terror, yet sympathies were seriously divided. Thomas Jefferson resigned as Washington's Secretary of State, to form a Republican party in opposition to the conservative Federalists. He and his Virginia colleague, James Madison, believed in the theory, if not the methods, of the revolution in France. Besides, they feared the potential of a strong one-party government in the

United States. Vice-President Adams was disturbed by the rift.

"Passions are as strongly excited now as before our revolution," he wrote John Quincy. "The foundations of the civilized world are in upheaval. . . . A man of your training and ability cannot in conscience remain out of politics."

John Quincy had already taken up his pen and joined the battle. In a series of articles published in the *Columbian Centinel* under the name "Publicola," he challenged the radical theories of Thomas Paine as set forth in his pamphlet titled "The Rights of Man." With vigor and perception, he revealed dangers and weaknesses in many of Paine's conclusions. In attacking Paine, he also attacked Tom Jefferson who had written the preface to the American edition. His arguments were so clearly stated and revealed such a broad understanding of political theory, that many thought the Vice-President himself was the author.

Having discovered his pen was mightier than his voice, he began to use it liberally, and with effect, in local issues. But when France declared war on Great Britain in 1795, he leaped again into the national—and international—arena.

Washington's government was hard-pressed by the widespread sympathy for France that threatened to involve the struggling, impoverished United States in a new war. France, in turn, expected her American ally to honor the Treaty of 1778. Under the pen names "Marcellus" and "Columbus," John Quincy attempted to cool the pro-French fever, urging strict neutrality in the present crisis. He pointed out that the new French administration was a collective autocracy as evil as the monarchy had been. For his own country, he feared war spelled disaster.

In the new executive offices at Philadelphia, George Washington read the articles with interest. They had already affected public opinion when his Proclamation of Neutrality was published throughout the states.

"The old alliance with His Most Christian Majesty," wrote Marcellus, "need not hold with the executioners of Louis XVI. . . ."

The President laid the newspaper on his desk and asked an orderly to summon his new Secretary of State, Edmund Randolph.

"I want you to look into the history of Mr. Adams' eldest son," he told Mr. Randolph. "These letters show a brilliant and logical mind, as well as an unusual grasp of the international situation. But don't tell our Vice-President what we're doing—not yet," he warned.

Within a few days, Secretary Randolph had the complete story of John Quincy's unusual education abroad, his diplomatic apprenticeship with both Mr. Dana and his father, his knowledge of languages as well as of law—especially international law.

"Everyone speaks highly of the young man's character and abilities," Randolph assured the President.

On May 29, 1794, George Washington sent this message to Congress: "I nominate John Quincy Adams to be Minister Resident to the Netherlands."

The nomination was unanimously confirmed the following day.

5

★★★★★★★★★★★★★★★★★★★★ **5** ★★★★★★★★★★★★★★★★★★★★

Diplomatic Tightrope

John Quincy Adams learned of his appointment as minister to the Netherlands from his father.

"I knew nothing of President Washington's plan to nominate you," Vice-President Adams assured his son. "He asked if I thought you would accept and I told him I would certainly advise you to do so."

Father and son were strolling through the familiar garden of the mansion. The fragrant June evening was filled with the muted sounds of sleepy birds, of small animals, and the faraway whisper of the sea.

"I would rather have built up my law practice and made some provision for my own fortune before taking on a public trust," John Quincy told his father. "But the experience will be worthwhile. I will give it a three-year trial. Then, if I have not been assigned a more important post, I can return to my practice without falling too far behind."

"The peaceful Netherlands that you recall is being torn apart between Britain and France," John Adams warned, "while republican sentiments have surely infected much of the citizenry. The post will require prudence. As representative to Stadholder William's government, you must not allow yourself to show any sympathy you might feel for the faction that would overthrow him. Keep your eyes open, and keep us informed of events there."

On his twenty-seventh birthday, July 11, 1794, John Quincy received his commission from Secretary of State Edmund Randolph at Philadelphia. Throughout that hot summer he perused State Department files, including six volumes of his father's dispatches from Europe and England, while he waited for the Secretary of the Treasury, Alexander Hamilton, to return from vacation. The financial condition of the United States was still shaky so one of his main jobs at The Hague was to obtain a new loan.

He was instructed in his general duties by Randolph and by the President, who invited the young minister to dine in his modest white house on Market Street. Mrs. Washington was intrigued by John Quincy's appearance.

"The resemblance to your father is striking," she told him, "but your nose and mouth—no they are more like your dear mother's, wouldn't you say so, George?"

The President would not commit himself, though the young man's stocky figure, already inclined to plumpness, was indeed much like Vice-President Adams'. Young Adams' face seemed to Washington to be open and honest—a handsome face with its finely molded nose, sensitive mouth and alert blue eyes beneath an unusually high forehead. The exquisite dress John Quincy had fancied at sixteen was replaced by smart but simple attire. He still powdered his hair, a custom many men were discarding.

"But it is already growing thin on top," President Washington remarked to his lady after their guest had departed.

"The poor lad will be bald as his father before he's forty, I fear.

On September 17, John Quincy sailed again out of Boston Harbor aboard the frigate *Alfred*. With him, as secretary, went his youngest brother, Thomas, a fledgling lawyer, and his father's valet, Tilly, a dour Englishman who had attached himself to Minister Adams when he was at the Court of St. James.

"He'll set you straight as to dress or protocol if ever you're in doubt," John Adams counseled. "Besides he's anxious to visit his mother who lives near London."

John Quincy was to travel to England to deliver important dispatches to John Jay, Chief Justice of the Supreme Court, whom Washington had sent as Envoy Extraordinary to negotiate a commercial treaty and settle problems arising out of Britain's war with France.

Members of the Crackbrain Club gave the brothers a hilarious send-off. Daniel Sargent and Nathan Frazier sailed with them as far as the light at the entrance to Massachusetts Bay, where the pilot boat would pick them up. Just before they hove to into the wind to discharge the pilot, Nathan drew John Quincy aside.

"I have never spoken to you about Mary," he told his friend, "but these years of waiting have been difficult with no word from you. She accepts the attentions of others with reservations. Daniel, for instance, would pay her court if he were certain you had no understanding . . ." Nathan's words trailed off into an embarrassed silence.

Mary, Mary . . . the memories welled back. John Quincy gripped the ship's rail and tried to answer evenly.

"Your sister is unusually favored by the gods, Nathan, with

wit and grace as well as beauty. I wish my future were more certain—"

The toot-toot of the pilot's whistle interrupted him. The ship was hauled into the wind with sails flapping. Daniel and Tommy were waving and shouting from the other side of the deck for Nathan to hurry.

"Certainly she could find no worthier suitor than Daniel. Tell her for me." John Quincy put his arm around Nathan's shoulders in a quick embrace. Then his friends were gone, over the side and down the rope ladder to the waiting sloop.

John Quincy watched by the rail until the pilot boat was a speck in the distance and the shores of Massachusetts Bay melded with the Atlantic. Must he always be a wanderer? Tommy's enthusiasm dispelled his loneliness until the ship bucked out into open sea. Then he spent much of the rough passage nursing his brother's *mal de mer*. Once again the ship proved leaky, but in less than a month the white cliffs of Dover loomed off their port bow.

Debarking before dawn on the beach at Deal, the young Americans immediately took a chaise for London, leaving Tilly to follow with the luggage. One trunk full of personal necessities and another with the dispatches for Ambassador Jay were strapped to the front of their coach.

"Don't take your eyes off the trunk full of papers," John Quincy warned Tommy. "They are instructions for Mr. Jay concerning his treaty negotiations. The British ministry would doubtless pay a spy well to get their hands on those instructions! So, in fact, would the French Directory who would like to prevent any treaty between Britain and the United States."

It was night before they reached London Bridge. The turnpike approach was so crowded that the travelers inched along, while John Quincy strained nervously watching the precious trunk. The clatter of the traffic was deafening, but just after paying the toll, he heard a rattling noise.

"Stop!" he called to the driver. "Did you hear that noise, Tommy?"

His brother was already out of the carriage. Shouting and waving his arms, Thomas managed to stop the coach behind them before its horses stumbled over one of the trunks that lay in the road. Several distressing moments passed before the other was located directly beneath their own carriage.

"Them trunks must 'ave been cut away," conjectured their driver, "for I 'ad strapped 'em tight for sure!"

"Be that as it may," replied John Quincy, "we'll carry them in the chaise with us the rest of the way."

So they swayed across the bridge and through the narrow London streets to the Virginia Coffee House, below the Royal Exchange, clutching both trunks on their laps.

"I would not give that coachman the satisfaction of knowing which trunk holds the dispatches," John Quincy whispered to Thomas. "I'm convinced that he knows more of this affair than you think!"

Tommy tried to reassure his brother that thieves could have cut the straps at the toll house, a common trick, but John Quincy's nerves were on edge. He went over and over the incident as they unpacked.

"Think of the mortification had they been lost! My career ruined before it even started!" He made a sudden decision. "I shall deliver the papers to Mr. Jay before I sleep."

So off he rode by hackney to the Royal Hotel in Pall Mall, still clutching the trunk. He found the forty-nine-year-old minister in bed suffering with rheumatism. The kindly face that John Quincy remembered well from both Paris and New

York was creased with pain, the thin mouth drawn and tense. But Mr. Jay greeted his young friend warmly, offering him a liqueur, inquiring about his family and asking eagerly for news from Philadelphia. The meeting was cordial though brief.

"But what if I'd had to tell Mr. Jay that I'd lost his instructions!" John Quincy mumbled as he fell into bed.

The streets of London were as dark, and the houses as drab, as John Quincy remembered them, but now he discovered a dazzling society hidden behind that forbidding exterior. For two weeks the brothers enjoyed a whirl of dinners and theater parties. They danced with a succession of lovely ladies whose Mammas were anxious to bring them to the attention of the distinguished American bachelors. John Quincy found the English women so fascinating that he vowed the sooner he left the country the better off he would be.

"But you missed meeting the loveliest ladies of all," Tommy assured him. He had dined that evening with the American consul, Joshua Johnson. "The house on Tower Hill is graced by seven charming daughters, three of whom," Thomas added pointedly, "are of marriageable age."

"I visited the Johnson's when they were in Nantes during the War for Independence," John Quincy recalled. "There were two or three girls then—just babies. I was sorry I could not accompany you this evening. Of course, I shall pay my respects. Poor man, with all those women to dress," he added absently, and turned back to the copy of Mr. Jay's treaty that he had been reading.

During his stay, the new minister had sat in on discussions of the treaty, which proved a liberal education in diplomatic realities. Hundreds of American ships engaged in trade with the French West Indies had been seized by the Royal Navy since the beginning of Britain's war with France. Determined to keep supplies from reaching her enemies, the "mistress of the seas" boarded and searched all neutral vessels, often appropriating them, their cargo, even their seamen.

At the same time, settlers in America's Northwest Territory had been terrified by rumors that the governor-general of Canada was inciting the Indians to attack them.

"Mr. Madison and the Republicans in Congress shout for retaliation," John Quincy told his brother, "but we cannot risk war. We need time to develop peacefully."

Thomas picked up the rough draft of the treaty. "According to this, we can trade only with British possessions, while allowing them to board and search our ships and seize property intended for her enemy! What happened to our principle 'free ships make free goods'?"

"Secretary Hamilton told me that much of our revenue comes from our trade with Britain and her possessions," John Quincy replied. "We must maintain good relations with this country. That's why the President sent John Jay to help the regular minister, Thomas Pinckney, work out a commercial treaty."

"I suppose it is better than war," Thomas said doubtfully.

His brother laughed. "That's exactly what Mr. Jay and Mr. Pinckney decided. Besides, His Majesty will withdraw all troops and garrisons from posts within our boundaries, while a joint commission will resurvey the Canadian boundary west of Lake of the Woods."

"Well that wilderness is only fit for Indians," scoffed Tommy.

John Quincy raised his eyebrows. "I wonder . . ."

When the Adams brothers arrived in the Netherlands at the end of October, the flat countryside seemed as placid as John Quincy had remembered it, its villages as swept and scrubbed. At The Hague, he presented his credentials to the Stadholder William, but by January, the Stadholder and his government and family had fled to England as the army of the French Directory marched across Holland on its frozen canals.

John Quincy was in Amsterdam on January 18 as the republican army approached. In the dark old streets, the tricolored cockades blossomed like tulips in the spring, and the walls shook with the martial strains of the "Marseillaise" as Dutch citizens prepared to welcome the invaders. Within days the Batavian Republic was established without resistance or violence.

"What do we do now?" asked Thomas.

"Wait for new instructions," John Quincy replied. "Meanwhile we will pay our respects to the "representans du peuple Francais.' "

Citizen Sieyès welcomed the "citoyen ministre" of the United States as the representative of a fellow republic and a neutral country.

"But it is rumored in Paris that the United States is negotiating a treaty with the British," the bald-headed little man reproached him.

"The public everywhere love to speculate, citizen," John Quincy reminded the Frenchman. "America is in a peculiar situation with regard to European conflicts—but no treaty has been ratified."

John Quincy soon became convinced that the "liberation" of the Netherlands in the name of brotherhood, equality and republicanism barely masked the French Directory's intention to establish a military dictatorship. It was impossible to raise the loan for which Secretary Hamilton hoped, since the

wealth of thrifty little Holland was being funneled into
yawning French coffers to support an army that was over-
running Europe. As one after another of Britain's Continental
allies sued for separate peace, John Quincy wrote his father:

"The French government avows peaceful intent, claiming
that they are only taking back what is rightfully theirs! They
may yet rule all Europe, and the final conflict with Britain
could be ruinous to our country. I hope that we may never
have occasion for political connections in Europe. We must
steel ourselves in unity."

But in the United States public opinion was torn between
sympathy for Britain and for France. Controversy over Mr.
Jay's treaty was bitter. Riots flared and speakers were stoned,
while President Washington and members of his government
were denounced by both sides for attempting to preserve
neutrality. Some of Washington's opponents even threatened
to impeach him.

Grumblings of dissension spanned the Atlantic. In The
Hague attempts were made, even on the part of his own
countrymen, to draw John Quincy into one faction or another. He remained neutral and on friendly terms with all
parties, until he was plunged into the political whirlpool by
orders to go to London to exchange ratifications of the controversial treaty. His instructions arrived in October, 1795,
too late for him to reach London on the date set.

"Doubtless the chargé d'affaires has transacted the business if Minister Pinckney is still in Spain as the orders indicate," he told his brother. "Perhaps I could consider my
responsibility at an end. The affair is unpleasant and unpromis-
ing," he sighed, "but I guess I have no election."

On arrival in London, John Quincy went directly to the
Hotel Osborne in the Strand where he had stayed twelve

years before while awaiting his mother and Nabby. After
breakfast, he walked through the familiar streets to Great
Cumberland Place, No. 1, to report to William Allen Deas,
the chargé d'affaires. The young man was out but a secretary
assured John Quincy that the treaty had been ratified on
schedule.

Freed of that responsibility, he breathed more deeply of
the sharp November air as he walked up Tower Hill to deliver
some letters to Joshua Johnson, the American consul.

Mr. Johnson greeted him with characteristic heartiness.
"Well you must dine with us this time," he told his fellow
American. "I'm hungry for news from home—news of your
father. We had many good talks in Nantes."

Johnson was an expatriate of long standing, having come
to London before the revolution as representative of an An-
napolis shipping firm, and he had married an Englishwoman.
When his brother, Thomas Johnson, signed the Declaration
of Independence—thus making England an impossible resi-
dence for Joshua—the Continental Congress made him Commissioner of Accounts in France where he and his family
lived out the war years.

"It would give me great pleasure to dine with you, and to
meet your family," he assured Johnson.

The young emissary returned to the embassy and was confronted with a strange dilemma when he discovered that the
British Foreign Office wished to confer on him a full commission as Minister Plenipotentiary. His Majesty's former
representative to the United States, George Hammond, whom
he had met in Philadelphia, told him frankly that he wished
Mr. Pinckney would go home.

"The place of minister here should be very agreeable to
you," Hammond insisted, "and you would be more acceptable

to the Foreign Secretary, my lord Grenville, and to the King. Besides, you would be succeeding to the station your father held."

"In my country," the young American replied acidly, "public office is not hereditary."

John Quincy thought Hammond shallow and treacherous, and found the British attempt to upgrade him embarrassing. He refused to be introduced to Lord Grenville or presented at court until it was understood that he was without portfolio —merely a stand-in for the regular minister.

A white-haired, enfeebled King George received the younger Adams in private audience. His mind was rumored to be failing, but he inquired cordially about John Adams and about his visitor's employment. Lord Grenville, however, was overbearing and irritatingly evasive during conferences to clarify certain points in Jay's treaty.

The British Navy continued to stop and board American ships seeking "contraband of war," a pretext to seize any cargo that suited them. A worse outrage was the pressing of American seamen into the service of the crown.

"Impressment is a great evil," Grenville admitted, "but a difficult question for both sides. If a sailor from one of His Majesty's ships deserts, it cannot be supposed that he thereby changes his allegiance or has automatically acquired the right to protection as an American citizen."

John Quincy knew his Blackstone—Bible of English law. He had argued this very question with Theophilus Parsons. His Lordship stood on firm ground according to British law.

"But Americans believe that a man has the right, for good cause, to put off his natural allegiance to the sovereign in whose land he was born," he reminded Grenville.

"Naturally," the British statesman sneered. "The law had

to be twisted to justify your revolution. But British law does not recognize such a right."

The admiralty did issue orders that men "regularly protected"—that is with certification of American citizenship—must not be impressed. In practice the order meant little. John Quincy was convinced that the retrieving of deserters was just one more excuse to interfere with America's burgeoning mercantile fleet. The young United States was becoming too great a power at sea.

The matter of evacuation of the northwest border posts was equally confounding. When pressed, Lord Grenville assured the emissary that orders had been made for that purpose. ". . . and I believe that they have been sent out," he stated flatly, but would not discuss the matter further.

"Obviously," John Quincy told William Deas, "the British intend to carry out the terms of the treaty only insofar as it suits them."

"Well, forget it for now," the young chargé d'affaires urged. "We've a dinner date on Tower Hill."

"What Are the United States?"

Dinner in the Johnson's gracious home beneath the Tower of London was a welcome change from diplomatic duties. The candelight twinkled on the heavy silver dinnerware and turned the crystal wine glasses into spectrums of color. John Quincy sipped the liquors gratefully, but it was the animated faces of his lovely young hostesses that warmed his heart.

Nancy and Louisa Catherine, the elder Johnson girls, were poised sophisticates, accustomed from childhood to the social world surrounding the courts of England and France. Schooled by their English mother, Catherine Nuth Johnson, their manners were impeccable. Counts and diplomats, princes or secretaries, all were received graciously in the Johnson's lively drawing room where conversation ranged from the arts and literature to politics, and was as often in French as in English.

"Strange I don't remember you at Nantes," John Quincy told the girls.

"Why should a boy of near twelve as you were then," laughed Nancy, "notice two little girls of six and four!"

John Quincy noticed them now. He was drawn irresistibly to their town house. Here he was certain of an attentive audience to whom he could air his views on any subject. Here, too, he brought his long-neglected flute and found enthusiastic accompaniment, for both Nancy and Louisa were accomplished musicians.

More and more his eyes sought the pixie face of the second daughter, Louisa Catherine.

"She is like a Romney portrait," he thought as he watched her playing the spinet one evening. Her brown curls were piled high above the delicate oval of her face, and her skin looked like cream velvet in the soft light from the tapers. Suddenly she turned, as if aware of his earnest gaze. She smiled, and the solemn concentration of the moment before was replaced by minxlike gaiety.

John Quincy felt an unfamiliar exhilaration as he moved to sit beside her on the spinet bench. The room behind them filled with chatter when the music stopped, but they might have been alone. He saw only the dark intelligent eyes that gazed at him questioningly, the delicate curve of her nose, the softness of her mouth. For once the worldly diplomat was speechless.

"What shall I play?" Louisa asked quietly, still smiling, but less certainly now, embarrassed by the intensity of his look. There was no trace of the rosebud smirk so fashionable with coquettes who found themselves admired, no fluttering eyelids, no giggle. Louisa stared right back at the handsome stranger, and it was he who dropped his eyes to the slender fingers lying on the spinet keys.

Not fully realizing what he was doing, John Quincy lifted her hands and held them in his upturned palms. Louisa was so startled by his unexpected gesture that she allowed them to lie there motionless while he studied their delicate perfection. How different they were from his mother's capable, work-hardened hands. How different was the world of Louisa Johnson from that in which John Quincy had grown to manhood. For her, the revolution was a faraway echo. Her patriotism remained untarnished by the realities of war and political controversy.

Nor had these hands ever known the day-to-day drudgery of a New England farm, but only the lightest of drawing-room tasks—sketching, needlework—the pursuits of a socialite, or of a diplomat's lady?

"I love you, Louisa," John Quincy told her a few weeks later. "I would be honored if you would be my wife. But," he warned, "I love my country more than life. My duty to the United States will always come before all other considerations."

Louisa was awed and fascinated by the solemn young diplomat. At times he seemed withdrawn, even morose. Yet he could be a gay, romantic companion who loved to dance until dawn. As a conversationalist, he shone in the most distinguished company. Certainly he was a welcome change from the vapid lazy dandies of London society. "Duty" as the wife of such a man meant, to twenty-one-year-old Louisa, hostessing in all the capitals of Europe. And who knew what honors the future might bring! It seemed certain that his father would succeed Washington as President. Her family agreed that the connection held the greatest promise.

In May, 1796, when John Quincy returned to The Hague no definite date had been set for his wedding.

"Louisa has been pampered with every luxury and refinement her father could afford," he told his brother. "She has no inkling what it would be like to exist on a minister's salary, especially here with wartime prices—not to mention other hazards to which I do not care to expose her."

That problem was solved when George Washington named John Quincy Minister Plenipotentiary to Lisbon, Portugal. The promotion doubled his salary to $9000, besides giving him a supplementary allowance for the change of posts. Sunny Portugal was a perfect spot to which to take a bride, as well as being a much cheaper place to live.

John and Abigail Adams did not greet the news of their son's engagement with enthusiasm. His mother frankly disapproved of his choice. She considered Louisa a "half-breed" as to nationality and felt Louisa's upbringing would not have fitted her for the trials that a diplomat's wife must face.

His father believed that John Quincy's career was not sufficiently established to undertake marriage. Foreign service depended on the fickle wind of politics. George Washington, wearied by determined opposition, would certainly not run again for the Presidency, nor was John Adams sure that he would be named to succeed him. No one could predict what course the young republic might take.

Even at twenty-nine, John Quincy heeded his parents' counsel when making important decisions, but, in love, he rode his own course. He wrote Louisa that they could be married the following summer before he took up his post in Lisbon. Only one problem still vexed him.

He wanted his father to be President with all his heart, believing no man more able or deserving. Yet how would such a circumstance affect his career, for he disliked the idea of holding a public office under his father no matter how merited? When he learned, early in 1797, that his father had indeed been elected to the nation's highest office, he wrote to his parents about his misgivings. John Adams, puzzled himself as to the proper course, sent John Quincy's letters to his predecessor. Washington's reply was prompt and decisive. He wrote:

> I thank you for giving me the perusal of the enclosed. The sentiments do honor to the head and heart of the writer, and if my wishes would be of any avail, they should go to you in a *strong hope* that you will not withhold merited promotion from Mr. John Adams because he is your son. . . . I give it as my decided opinion that Mr. Adams is the most valuable public character we have abroad, and that . . . he will prove himself the ablest of all our diplomatic corps.

In May, President Adams asked the Senate to reassign his son to a new embassy being established at Berlin, a post he considered more important than Lisbon. A treaty signed in 1785 with Prussia was about to expire and the United States wanted essential changes incorporated into the renewal to make it conform with Jay's treaty. Neutral Prussia would doubtless balk at giving up any commercial freedom on the seas even temporarily.

On a bright July evening in 1797, a courier brought news of the change of post to the dock at Maasluys, where John Quincy and Thomas were boarding a boat to England for the wedding. The groom walked the deck most of the night, wondering how he could tell Louisa. A bridal cottage had been rented in Lisbon, and many of his furnishings, including his precious library—a small but careful selection of classics collected over the past five years—had been shipped directly from The Hague.

Louisa's father, though unable to furnish a dowry due to business reverses caused by the war, had fitted out the cabin space of one of his company's ships to transport the bridal couple down the coast. Now all these fond preparations must be changed, at an expense neither groom nor father could well afford.

"Why Prussia is hardly civilized!" gasped Louisa, echoing a prevalent opinion of the German kingdom. "And not even a house prepared for us!" The idealistic bride with her dreams of gracious hostessing in a lavish embassy was experiencing her first taste of that "duty" which ruled her husband's life.

"Berlin is a modern city. I saw it being built only fifteen years ago," John Quincy reminded her. "I am told that the German people are very industrious. Certainly their art and music indicate a measure of civilization, and, while German literature is not well known here, I understand it is worth studying."

"Doubtless we'll manage," Louisa conceded, "but all the lovely clothes I bought for Portugal will be quite unsuitable in that cold climate!"

On the evening of July 26, 1797, John Quincy made one terse entry in his diary:

> At nine this morning I went, accompanied by my brother, to Mr. Johnson's, and thence to the Church of the parish of All Hallows Barking, where I was married to Louisa Catherine Johnson, the second daughter of Joshua and Catherine Johnson, by Mr. Hewlett. Mr. Johnson's family, Mr. Brooks, my brother, and Mr. J. Hall were present. We were married before eleven in the morning, and immediately after went out to see Tilney House, one of the splendid country seats for which this country is distinguished.

The bridegroom was solemn and proud as he and Thomas watched the dainty bride in her high-waisted ruffled dress approach down the aisle of the ancient church of All Hallows. Louisa held her lovely head high, conscious that she was marrying the most eligible bachelor in her world, scion of one of America's most distinguished families, son of the President of the United States.

Between posts, John Quincy had, for once in his life, complete leisure to enjoy his dear new companion. But as the moment to depart for Prussia drew near, Louisa became nervous. To add to her apprehension, her father had decided to leave England, where it was becoming difficult for an American shipper to do business, and seek haven in his native Maryland.

"A million miles from Berlin!" his daughter wailed.

So it was a bride already fretful from worry and lack of sleep whom John Quincy and his brother took aboard ship late in October, 1797, for the trip across the North Sea to Hamburg. Louisa was dreadfully ill throughout the stormy eight-day passage.

Once on land, Louisa rallied to enjoy the sightseeing. In Hamburg, they met the Swedish minister who told them that old Frederick Wilhelm II was dying. There was no need to hurry on to Berlin, as John Quincy might have to wait months, as in the Netherlands, for credentials to a new government.

During a week's stay in Hamburg, John Quincy met several times with a group of Americans and French émigrés who were trying to obtain the release of the Marquis de Lafayette from the Austrian prison where he had been since 1792. John Quincy donated a sum he could ill afford to aid his old friend.

During the first day of the overland trip to Berlin, Louisa was buoyed by curiosity. The postilions who rode the lead horse of every chaise particularly fascinated her. Each wore a French horn about his shoulders, which he blew enthusiastically at every opportunity, sending cattle, poultry and peasants tumbling away from the thundering hooves of the huge coach horses.

But five days in the wooden-wheeled, springless carriages, swaying and bumping across the rutted roads of Prussia, reduced Louisa to a weeping, sickly woman.

The Americans arrived at the Brandenburg Gate about 1:00 P.M. on November 7. They were stopped by a dapper young lieutenant of the guards.

"Who are you?" he asked.

Thomas had stepped down from the coach and he announced in his most authoritative voice and his best German:

"The Minister of the United States! The United States of America!"

The officer fingered his mustache thoughtfully as he examined their papers. He muttered in German, "I do not understand. What are the United States, please?" He shrugged his shoulders helplessly.

Both Tommy and his brother were puzzled as to how to explain in their limited German when a guard plucked at the officer's sleeve. Evidently the soldier had heard of the United States, for after a hurried conversation, the lieutenant returned, all smiles.

"Forgive the delay, Mein Herr Minister. In these days, one cannot be too careful. I will have you escorted into the city." He shook hands all around and, bowing smartly, sped them on their way.

By the time the Adamses were finally settled in the Hotel de Russie, Louisa had a raging fever. With all Berlin's attention directed to the palace where the King lay dying, the hotel manager had difficulty finding a doctor. The one who finally came spoke no English, nor did the nurse whom he sent to care for his patient. After making Louisa comfortable, they somehow conveyed the sad news that she had been pregnant and had lost the baby. Too weak to cry, Louisa turned her wan face to the wall and mourned silently. John Quincy vented his disappointment by throwing himself into his work.

The following day, he requested an audience with Count Finkenstein, the eldest of Prussia's three foreign ministers, who knew the American ambassador by reputation. When the old King died within the week, his son, Frederick Wilhelm III, received John Quincy immediately, according him temporary recognition pending receipt of his amended credentials.

"I am indebted to Count Finkenstein for clearing away all the trash of diplomatic ceremony," John Quincy told his brother. "The young King is a forthright soldier who has assured me of his earnest desire to maintain the friendly connection with the United States."

Within the hour, further evidence of cordiality came with a summons from the bereaved Dowager Queen, requesting that he wait on her that very afternoon. Her Majesty welcomed him like an old friend, asking eagerly for news of her daughter whom he had met at The Hague. The Princess of Orange was married to one of Stadholder William's sons and had fled with him to England when the French marched into the Netherlands. Satisfied that all was well with them, the old Queen inquired about the minister's bride.

"My Louisa is very ill, Your Majesty," John Quincy confessed. "The journey was difficult."

The Queen Mother summoned a servant immediately. "My own physicians must attend her," she declared, and instructed the footman to send for them.

One of them, Dr. Brown, an Englishman, reassured the

mournful patient that her care had been adequate and no lasting harm had been done.

"Just rest and get well, my dear," he told Louisa, "and don't fret. You are young and may still be blessed with many children."

Dr. Brown sent an English maid to tend Louisa and a few days later found more comfortable lodgings for the Americans. The apartment was beautifully situated overlooking the Tiergarten near the Brandenburg Gate, almost over the guard house where they had been detained on arrival. The rolling drums, the trampings and challengings of the guards outside the window, were an irritation to Louisa night and day. Still the apartment was all they could find in Berlin at a price they could afford, and she grew stronger every day despite the annoying sound effects.

Soon the parades and fanfare began to amuse her. On sunny days, the Americans strolled down the Unter den Linden to inspect the imposing palaces and public buildings. Within a few months, they were caught up in a whirl of gaiety that centered around the young King and his beautiful Queen Louisa.

The Queen greeted her American namesake warmly, and they became close friends. The Adamses became intimate with the King's cousin, Princess Anton Radziwell and her charming Polish husband. They were kindred spirits, not only in their enthusiasm for the republican government in America, but in their love of all the arts. The Princess acted as a willing guide for Louisa through the maze of court protocol.

John Quincy finally found a house on the corner of the Friedrichstrasse and the Behrenstrasse that their congressional allowance could afford. Louisa added a few tasteful second-hand pieces to the sparse furnishings. Though she never ceased to complain about their "niggling" salary, her charm and ingenuity made her receptions and little dinners in their modest home a unique attraction to the nobles and sophisticates of Berlin who were accustomed to lavish display. And Louisa happily attended all the brilliant court festivities, escorted by Tommy when business detained her husband.

Work on the treaty could not begin until summer of 1798 when John Quincy's new credentials arrived. He used the time to establish cordial relations with the Prussian ministers.

The talks went forward in perfect good will and friendliness. As an ally of Great Britain, Prussia was already resigned to curtailing her overseas trade and allowing the British the right of visit and search for the duration of her war against Napoleon. Still the negotiations consumed a full year. Thomas became ill and returned home, accompanied by the valet, Tilly. So John Quincy himself had to rewrite the documents three times and make fair copies before the treaty was finally signed on July 11, 1799, his thirty-second birthday. Then John Quincy took his bride on a tour of Prussia.

The trip was a true second honeymoon. They went sightseeing in the mountains, and Louisa was carried up the Geyersberg in a sedan chair. They floated down the Elbe in a raft. They lingered in Dresden where they found decent hotels, friends who were also vacationing and a continual festival of art and fine music.

While they vacationed, the world trembled on the brink of new disaster. The First Consul of France Napoleon Bonaparte returned from Egypt determined to crush British power. The little Corsican dreamed of uniting all Europe under France—with himself as Emperor.

Across the sea, John Quincy's father found it more and more difficult to maintain neutrality. With George Washington's death his party split asunder, and went down to defeat. In 1800, Republican Thomas Jefferson was elected President, and John Adams recalled his son from Berlin.

The note of recall arrived on April 26, 1801.

"The objects of your mission to Berlin having been entirely accomplished," wrote John Marshall, Secretary of State, "the President is of the opinion that you may be permitted to return to the United States."

"Oh dear, must we go?" asked Louisa, already knowing the answer.

They must leave their warm friends and court life to return to a land almost as strange to John Quincy after six years' absence, as to expatriate Louisa. What could be his future there?

They would return to a depleted family circle, for John Quincy's brother Charles had died the year before. But John Quincy's chief worry was still Louisa's health—plus a new and welcome concern.

"I travel," he wrote Thomas, "with a wife whom I tenderly love in such a state of health, and with a child three weeks old—a long-expected, ardently desired, painfully born and only child. I ought not to complain, but the prospect of my return is a view to which I look forward with profound anxiety...."

The baby, born on April 12, 1801, was named George Washington Adams. The father confessed doubt as to the wisdom of giving "a great and venerable name to such a lottery ticket as a newborn infant." The gesture was no mere token in respect to the great man's public character. As John Quincy explained, "President Washington was, next to my own father, the man upon earth to whom I was indebted for the greatest personal obligations."

7

★★★★★★★★★★★★★★★★★★★★★ 7 ★★★★★★★★★★★★★★★★★★★★★

The "Unmanageable"
Mr. Adams

◢

John Quincy introduced his wife and small son to their native land in September of 1801.

Landing at Philadelphia, he hired a carriage to take Louisa and George to her family's home in Frederick, Maryland. The green countryside of Pennsylvania and Maryland dotted with neat farms, fat cattle and prosperous farmers surprised Louisa.

"I half thought America was mostly forest and Indians!" she told her husband. "Why it's more beautiful than England —or any part of Europe!"

In contrast to the countries of Europe, depressed by decades of revolution and war, they saw everywhere the marks of peace—new roads, new homes, new public buildings.

John Quincy left Louisa and George at Frederick as he was anxious to see his own parents. He found the aging former President disillusioned and fearful for the future of the republic with that "radical" Jefferson as President. His mother was bitter in defeat.

"Those Republicans called your father a tyrant!" she told her son. "They even suggested that he wished to make himself king. How could the people forget so soon! The United States would have been stillborn but for the work and sacrifice of men like your father."

Both grieved for Charles whose hearty voice would never again echo in the high-ceilinged rooms of the old mansion. John Quincy's return delighted them, and when Louisa arrived with George, Abigail Adams took her daughter-in-law to her heart, all doubts of her worthiness dispelled. Once more the house was abustle, and the rooms that had seemed too big and empty rang again with the lusty cries of an Adams baby.

With his meager savings, John Quincy bought and furnished a home at 39 Hanover Street in Boston and opened a law office in State Street. At thirty-four, it was difficult to start over, especially as many of his juniors were already well established. Besides, his attention was drawn irresistibly to public affairs. In January, 1802, two months after settling in Boston, he complained in his diary:

> I feel strong temptation and have great provocation to plunge into political controversy, but I hope to preserve myself from it. A politician in this country must be the man of a party. I would fain be the man of my whole country.

Like his ideal statesman, George Washington, John Quincy disapproved of the party system. He could not adhere fully to the principles of either party. He thought of himself as a Federalist in that he believed in a strong central government taking precedent over the rights of the states when the two conflicted. Yet now that the Republicans were in power, they were going farther than the Federalists in the exercise of federal power and in defending the Constitution.

"Mr. Jefferson said: 'We are all Republicans, we are all Federalists,'" John Quincy mused aloud to Louisa as they sat before the fire that January night. "Easy for a President to say, but could a practical politician make it work?"

Louisa smiled over her needlework. She had no idea that her Johnny could remain out of the political arena. They might yet live in Washington near her family. How she detested cold New England!

The Boston Federalists elected John Quincy to represent them in the Massachusetts Senate in April, 1802. Immediately he manifested an independence that startled his conservative colleagues. His first act was to move that proportionate representation on the governor's council be given the Republican minority, considered "rabble" by the Federalists. Then he voted against a new bank in Boston because its charter proposed a closed corporation for "gentlemen of respectable character."

The powerful banking interests easily won their charter, but the presumptuous new senator protested to the end that the stock should be open to all Massachusetts citizens.

". . . as if the size of a man's bankroll is the measure of his respectability!" grumbled John Quincy.

The Federalist party did appear overweighted with the privileged, the wealthy—and too confined to the northeast section of the country. Some party leaders considered John Quincy "unmanageable."

"This man is not our friend," editorialized the *Independent Chronicle*.

Despite his lack of party discipline, most Federalists recognized his abilities. In November, 1802, his district nominated him to represent them in the United States House of Representatives and, in the final vote, he was defeated by only a narrow margin. It was a lucky defeat, for in February, 1803, the Massachusetts legislature appointed him over veteran Timothy Pickering to represent them in the United States Senate.

That July 4, Louisa bore a second son whom they named John. While John Quincy became acquainted with the new baby, world events were shaping a political situation which would mark him as a party renegade on his first vote as U.S. senator.

When Napoleon Bonaparte conquered Spain, he claimed her vast empire in the New World, including Florida, New Orleans and the Louisiana Territory. Taking advantage of a truce with England, he was preparing to occupy the rich Mississippi Valley. Control of the river would give France a powerful influence in the American West.

President Jefferson instructed his minister at Paris, Robert Livingston, to try to buy the vital port of New Orleans and the territory of West Florida adjacent to it. Before special envoy James Monroe reached Paris, Napoleon decided to sell the whole Louisiana Territory. The task of occupying the faraway wilderness was overwhelming, especially as renewed war with Great Britain seemed imminent. The cash offered was more inviting.

On April 30, 1803, Monroe and Livingston put their signatures to the biggest land transaction in history—the Louisiana Purchase. The United States acquired some 885,000 square miles—doubling its territory—for $15,000,000. The "noble bargain" was ratified by Congress in special session on October 17.

Only a small group of New England Federalists dissented. They feared the growth of the West and South—largely agrarian and Republican—which inevitably spelled doom to

Federalist influence in national politics. Some even spoke of secession.

At twilight on October 20, the new Federalist senator from Massachusetts rode into Washington with his wife, and two sons, three days too late to cast his vote on the Louisiana Purchase Bill. In the rutted mud that passed for a road in the "Capital City," they almost collided with the carriage of an old Massachusetts friend, Samuel Otis, secretary of the Senate. He shouted greetings to the Adamses.

"What delayed you, John!" he cried. "The purchase treaties have been approved, twenty-four to seven. I've just delivered the resolution of 'advise and consent' to the President."

"We've been three weeks on the way," John Quincy replied, "with illness and delays of every sort. No matter. My vote would have changed nothing."

Washington was a desolate malarial swamp where the few brick buildings were scattered amidst scrubby brush. The President's House stood on a rise of ground, handsome—and quite alone. The unfinished Capitol stood on another hill, nearly two miles away. Between was a jumble of unkempt boarding houses where the legislators huddled together, miserable in temporary bachelorhood. Few would expose their wives to the discomforts of the raw settlement that was the seat of government.

The Adamses were more fortunate, for they were to live with Louisa's sister Nancy, now Mrs. Walter Hellen. Louisa was soon caught up in a gay group that surrounded her mother and father, now commissioner of stamps, with a home on K Street, near the Georgetown Bridge. Four-year-old George found a playmate in his cousin Johnson Hellen, while baby John's cradle rocked cozily beside that of his cousin Mary.

Their father's official welcome was not so warm. In the

Senate, the Republicans lorded it over the Federalists, who turned their frustrated wrath on the younger Adams. His father, many felt, had caused their downfall. John Quincy fanned their resentment by supporting the acquisition of Louisiana and voting the necessary bonds for its purchase. He was the only New England Federalist to do so.

"The loss of influence of our section is more than compensated for by the extension of national power," he declared. "This republic is a robust infant. Expansion is both desirable and inevitable." Influential Federalists like Alexander Hamilton agreed, but John Quincy had no doubt of the enmity he had roused. On the last day of the year 1803, he noted in his diary:

> My election as a Senator of the United States, for six years, has been the only important incident of my political career. It will probably affect very materially my future situation in life. I have already had occasion to experience, what I had before the fullest reason to expect, the *danger* of adhering to my own principles. The country is so totally given up to the spirit of party, that not to follow blindfold the one or the other is an inexpiable offence. . . . I see the impossibility of pursuing the dictates of my own conscience without sacrificing every prospect, not merely of advancement, but even of retaining that character and reputation I have enjoyed. Yet my choice is made, and, if I cannot hope to give satisfaction . . . I am at least determined to have the approbation of my own reflections.

In January, 1804, John Quincy fought the Republicans' Louisiana revenue bill.

"The Senate has no right to tax the people of that territory without their consent any more than the British parliament had a right to tax the colonies," he told Timothy Pickering, who had followed him to Washington as junior senator.

The older man, angered at being displaced by an "upstart"

like Adams, was to prove a jealous adversary rather than a partner. He voted for the revenue bill against his colleague's resolutions, though he was on record as disapproving everything else about the Louisiana Purchase.

"So much for Mr. Pickering," shrugged John Quincy.

The same month, he further shocked the Federalists by attending the Louisiana celebration feast at Stelle's public house with the President and his department heads and about seventy members of Congress—all Republicans.

"The dinner was bad," John Quincy complained when he returned home soon after eight, "and the toasts were too numerous. I cannot see why that tavern is so popular!"

"Most congressmen are not spoiled by Continental cuisine," teased Nancy Hellen. "Was Mr. Jefferson in good spirits?"

"He told his usual quota of tall tales," her brother-in-law answered sleepily.

The young Federalist senator was resented because of his friendship with the Republican President. The Adamses had been in Washington less than three weeks when Tom Jefferson invited them to one of his informal dinners. The simplicity of the shambling, freckle-faced widower shocked many legislators accustomed to the more formal Federalist administrators. Even when Abigail and John Adams had moved from the metropolis of Philadelphia to the unfinished President's House in Washington, they had tried to maintain the social amenities of the Presidency.

Jefferson often appeared at state dinners in old clothes and carpet slippers. He observed no precedence in seating, letting his guests scramble for a place at table—and to that table he invited whomever he pleased. In the case of John Quincy Adams, he apparently chose to forget the rift with the father, and the son's own barbed attack on him in the letters of "Publicola," remembering only the close association of earlier years.

"Mr. Jefferson is a practical politician," John Quincy told Louisa as they drove home from the President's House. "There must be good reason for his friendliness."

"Well, he certainly does tell large stories," she remarked. "Surely he never learned Spanish in nineteen days by reading *Don Quixote!*"

"Nor have temperatures in Paris ever reached twenty degrees below zero for one day. Yet I heard him say he saw Fahrenheit's thermometer register thereabouts for six weeks!" John Quincy shook his head. "He knows better than all this, but he loves to excite wonder. Still, make no mistake, the President is a brilliant man—and a good musician too. Next time we'll ask him to play his violin for you."

John Quincy was in agreement with many of the Republican President's views and policies. Early in the Massachusetts senator's second session, Jefferson confided to him his concern over increased impressment of American seamen by British warships.

"They have become bolder since they are fighting France again," Jefferson told Adams. "Why, they stop our ships within sight of land!"

"They might as well send officers from Canada to recruit forcibly on United States soil!" John Quincy averred. "But service in the Royal Navy is 'floating Hell,' what with the floggings and the filthy food. Death and disease take as many men as desertion, so they must constantly replenish their ranks. Besides they feel justified in taking our men." Briefly he outlined his talks on the subject with Lord Grenville.

"No more than a fraction of the impressed sailors can be deserters!" The President shook his head. "They are no more justified than the traders who kidnap Africans to sell into slavery. I intend to put a stop to both!"

Jefferson's sandy hair was streaked with gray, his strong face lined with the cares of his office. Because of the Louisiana Purchase, secession was openly planned by a group of extreme Federalists called the Essex Junto. Even the Vice-President, Aaron Burr, though a Republican, was suspected of conspiring to lead his state of New York out of the Union to join the "Northern Confederacy." In July, he had killed Alexander Hamilton in a duel when the former Secretary of Treasury accused him of treason.

"So a man under indictment for murder is presiding as president of the Senate of the United States!" John Quincy exclaimed after the opening of Congress on November 5, 1804. "Our overseas trade is threatened by both Britain and France; our union threatened by selfish interests at home. No wonder Mr. Jefferson feels overburdened with worry!"

Early in 1805, John Quincy moved a resolution to levy a tax on the importation of slaves, hoping to discourage the inhuman traffic. The motion was voted down with hardly a fight.

Despite his feeble political power, the Senate soon discovered that their unpredictable member had a tremendous capacity for work. He was named to one committee after another. He sponsored a drive to set up a Library of Congress and succeeded in procuring an annual appropriation and a room to house the first sparse collection of volumes.

With an eye to westward expansion, he considered it important to have a committee of three investigate a proposed boundary adjustment with British America. The northeast and northwest boundaries had been left open since the Treaty of Peace and Independence of 1783. Now the British wished the western boundary to be set on a line from Lake of the Woods to the source of the Mississippi.

At the time of the Louisiana Purchase, President Jefferson sent Meriwether Lewis and William Clark to gather geographical facts about the new territory. In 1805, Lieutenant Zebulon Montgomery Pike traveled from St. Louis up the Mississippi, seeking its source. Neither party actually reached the river's headwaters.

As spokesman for the boundary committee, John Quincy argued to eliminate the article settling the northwest boundary until more information could be obtained.

"Such a settlement might allow British territory to come too far south," he insisted.

Secretary of State James Madison was inclined to give the British their way. Like John Quincy's brother, Thomas—and indeed, most Americans—he was of the opinion that the area was valuable only to Indians and trappers. Congress, however, did vote to cut the controversial article from the convention.

"For once they listened to me," John Quincy exulted in the privacy of his family, "which is a triumph in itself!"

The difference of opinion over the boundary affected in no way the mutual respect and warm friendship that had developed between the Adamses and the Madisons. John Quincy and Louisa dined often with "Little Jemmy" and his vivacious wife Dolley.

"I wish I had one-tenth her energy," Louisa sighed after her first meeting with Mrs. Madison.

Louisa complained often of being unwell. Her boys consumed much of her meager energy. Yet in Washington, as in Berlin, she shone as a hostess, and held regular social gatherings to which residents of the bleak capital thronged.

Louisa presided over her "salons" charmingly, but her husband was a stiff host. He talked with animation at small gatherings and enjoyed an evening of cards or chess with friends, but he hated the semi-public affairs.

"I cannot make small talk," he excused himself, when Louisa scolded him for being cold, "and am tongue-tied when confronted in my own living room by a senator who has just vilified me in the Senate!"

He preferred his quiet routine—rising at seven, reading, writing or playing with George until breakfast at nine. Summer and winter he walked the two and one-half miles to the Capitol, a distance he covered in forty-five minutes. The Senate sat until 2:00 or 3:00 P.M. When adjournment was earlier, John Quincy often listened to debates in the House of Representatives. Political controversy fascinated him now as diplomatic sparring had intrigued him at seventeen.

After dinner at four, he played with the babies—his John and his niece, Mary Hellen—or read to his son George and nephew Johnson Hellen before they were put to bed. Evenings he read light literature to the ladies or listened to them play on spinet and harp until supper at nine. Bedtime was early when they were at home, for John Quincy was fatigued by the pressures and antagonisms in the Senate.

The Federalists still considered him "unmanageable" while the Republicans had some reason to be satisfied with his performance. But to try to secure him in either camp was like trying to grasp quicksilver.

"The senior senator from Massachusetts votes on every measure as if it were a proposition in Euclid," one colleague observed, "with no regard for party considerations!"

John Quincy Adams considered the judgment a compliment.

8

Atlas Unshaken

Each summer, the Adamses fled the heat of Washington to enjoy the sea breezes of Braintree. There John Quincy had purchased the old farmstead at Penn's Hill. Among family and friends, the days were relaxed and pleasant, devoted to study, swimming, gardening or riding across the familiar fields. Old John Adams listened endlessly to the political news from Washington, criticizing freely the trends of government. By 1806, he was especially concerned with his son's part in them.

The renewed war between Britain and France was seriously affecting American shipping. Napoleon had closed European ports to English ships and neutral ships that came from British ports. The British fleet, having destroyed the French Navy at Trafalgar in 1805, patrolled the sea lanes of the world unmolested. Her particular interest in keeping American ship-owners from trading with the French West Indies had brought the war to the very coastal waters of North America.

During the winter of 1806, Congress sought means to stop the ship seizures. In February, John Quincy introduced a set of resolutions condemning British aggressions. They asked that the President demand restoration of, or payment for, confiscated property. Both resolutions were carried, but by Republican votes. Many Federalists were traders and ship-masters. Though they were losing millions in goods and ships and thousands of seamen to the British, yet they opposed Republican attempts to retaliate. Their trade was risky but still profitable.

In April, John Quincy backed Jefferson's Non-Importation Act, openly aligning himself against his own party. When he went home for the summer recess, his father reproached him for his stand.

"I suppose you realize you may be committing political suicide by backing Republican measures," he warned.

But Abigail Adams was proud of her son's independence. "Your father was not so cautious about embargoes when we banned British tea!" she reminded them both.

It was John Quincy's health that worried his mother.

"Louisa tells me that you have frequent colds in winter," she remonstrated. "Even now you have a persistent cough."

"Well, I have given up smoking since reading Ben Water-house's pamphlet on its dangers," John Quincy admitted. "It took me months to rid myself of the habit, though t'was not so difficult for me to start—as you remember."

"No, he works too hard," Louisa insisted. "He walks to the Capitol in the coldest weather, and I'm sure he's the last to leave the Senate chamber to seek the fires in the anteroom!"

"You must not let the mind wear so much on the body," his mother admonished. "I'm sure that you eat too little and study too much."

Yet, when she found him digging happily in the garden, unshaven and in old clothes, a frayed farmer's hat protecting his balding, unpowdered head, she expressed shock at his relaxed appearance.

"Now, I hope you never appear in the Senate with a beard two days old," she scolded, "or otherwise look shabby!"

That June, 1806, John Quincy was installed as professor of rhetoric and oratory at Harvard—the first such course in the country. Though he felt deficient as an extemporaneous speaker, his confidence grew when he saw how well his lectures were received by the scholars.

"I enjoy working with those young men," he told his father. "Several of them show oratorical promise—especially young Edward Everett."

Because of his senatorial duties, he taught only the summer and fall terms, but during the summer he purchased a new home in Boston, on Nassau Street at the corner of Frog Lane, overlooking the Common.

"We might as well have a home here," he decided. "I see no prospect for myself in public service when my term as senator expires in 1809."

"You make a fine professor," Louisa told him, happily anticipating a settled home at last—though Washington would have suited her better than cold Boston. "I hear rumors that you may be asked to serve as president of Harvard."

"The prospect of devoting myself to scholarly pursuits is not unpleasing," John Quincy admitted.

In November when he returned to Washington a bill to prohibit the slave trade was introduced. To John Quincy the institution of slavery was an "abscess on the national body," but he took no part in the debates on the subject. Slavery of another sort commanded his attention—the impressment of American seamen into service on His Britannic Majesty's warships.

The last step in a series of outrages occurred on a June night in 1807, in the peaceful waters off the Virginia Capes. The U.S.S. *Chesapeake*, sailing out of Norfolk, was hailed by H.M.S. *Leopard* off Cape Henry at the entrance to Chesapeake Bay. The *Chesapeake*'s captain, Commodore James Barron, signaled that his ship was a frigate of the United States Navy—not subject to search. The *Leopard* opened fire.

Unprepared as she was to do battle, the *Chesapeake* quickly struck her colors. Three American sailors had been killed and eighteen wounded, including Commodore Barron. The British boarded the gunboat and seized four seamen, prodding them into their longboat with bayonets. With the guns of the *Leopard* trained on them, the American crew could only stare helplessly.

At dawn one of the impressed sailors was hung from the yardarm, a grisly warning to any who dared oppose the Queen of the Seas.

John Quincy was in Boston when he heard the news. Livid with rage, he paced his study floor.

"How can we fight back?" he repeated over and over to wide-eyed young George who had brought in the paper. "No navy—no army—damn, I say damn!"

Suddenly he rushed hatless into the street and down to State Street, to the office of John Lowell, leader of the Boston Federalists.

"We must register a strong protest against this outrage," he shouted at the surprised shipowner. "I have been from the first strongly opposed to any encroachment on American rights by the British—or any other foreign power! Now see how they use us, sir!"

Lowell's fat face grew red as he lifted his imposing bulk from behind his desk and walked to the window.

"And see, sir, what your Non-Importation Act has done!" Lowell pointed to the harbor which was crowded with tall-masted ships that dared not leave its shelter. "T'is that Republican Jefferson that's driving Britain to molest our ships—crippling our trade with his warlike measures!" The merchant turned on John Quincy. "And you, sir, have no better sense than to support him."

"Have you no interest in protecting your seamen?" asked John Quincy.

"They have every right to rout out deserters," roared Lowell, "—craven cowards who hope to avoid their duty to defend their country!"

John Quincy was astounded to hear impressment thus defended, but he held his temper. "Our navy should certainly not enlist deserters," he conceded. "But the sailors from the *Chesapeake*, save for the one already hung, are native Americans; their papers were quite in order."

John Lowell blew like a cresting porpoise. "Really, my dear Adams," he sputtered, "anyone can acquire a 'cradle' certificate for a dollar. Dozens of hags along the coast make their living by swearing they borned this flotsam of the sea! I doubt not that the number of legitimate Americans taken this way is infinitesimal."

"If the number never exceeded a single one," John Quincy replied evenly, though his voice threatened to crack with anger, "t'would be too many. The rights of that one would be no less vital, the offense against the civilized usages of nations no less heinous."

On July 10, John Quincy attended a citizen's meeting where he was named to a committee of seven to draw up strong protest resolutions. No other Federalist was present.

"I shall have my head taken off for apostasy to the party,"

he told Louisa next evening. "But this day I am forty years old, and too set in my ways to begin yielding my sense of duty to party considerations."

Louisa smiled at her husband's troubled face. Lines of care were beginning to show around his eyes and mouth. Without wig or powder, the sparseness of his hair was very evident, and the few strands left were more gray than golden. She pulled herself from her rocker—with difficulty because of the child she would soon bear—and went to perch on the arm of his chair. John Quincy took her hand and pulled her into the big wing chair beside him.

"I'm becoming a cantankerous old man, my dearest. How do you put up with me? When I reflect how much I have received in blessings from Heaven, and how little I return that can benefit the world . . ."

Louisa put her finger to his lips, and kissed him gently on the forehead.

In August Louisa blessed the new house on Nassau Street with a third son. They named the boy Charles Francis, for John Quincy's dead brother and for Judge Dana with whom he had traveled to Russia.

That same month, Robert Fulton made a steamboat voyage from New York to Albany—150 miles up the Hudson River in thirty-two hours. All Washington was agog about the new invention when Congress reconvened that fall.

"I think his torpedoes a valuable invention too," President Jefferson opined at dinner one evening. "Their destructive effect appears certain—and devastating."

John Quincy thought the President must be giving serious thought to rebuilding an effective navy. For the time being, however, the administration asked Congress for a stringent embargo on all American shipping, which forbade trade with any foreign nation. Though John Quincy realized that the bill would cause hardship—even a depression if it remained in effect for long—he served on the committee that drew up the bill. Then he helped rush it through both houses before defiant captains could flee the closed ports.

New England Federalists were roused to a new pitch of fury, while members of the Essex Junto cried "secede!" more loudly than ever. Senator Adams bore the brunt of their frustrated wrath because of his part in the bill.

Even Louisa, who never interfered in political affairs, wrote her husband from Quincy:

"Your father was much concerned about the bill which passed so rapidly through the Senate, and still cannot account for the vote of a certain friend of mine. . . . He has taxed me once or twice before. These votes he says he never can forgive."

"This embargo is no more a favorite of mine than non-importation," John Quincy wrote Governor Sullivan of Massachusetts, "but, besides avoiding exposing to capture any vessels issuing from port, it may even curtail impressment, since unemployed British sailors would soon return to their own ships in order to draw pay. Yet I hope some expedient will be devised to remove existing restrictions on our trade."

By 1808, John Quincy's standing in the Senate was as distinguished as it had been humble in the beginning. Yet, on most national questions he was led to support the administration. In June, the Massachusetts Federalists elected his successor nine months before the end of his term. The party further rebuked him by adopting strong resolutions against the Embargo Bill which he had backed. Then they made his situation intolerable by drawing up a list of instructions to guide their representatives' votes. Senator Adams submitted his letter of resignation.

". . . to hold my seat in the Senate of the United States without exercising the most perfect freedom of agency, under the sole and exclusive control of my own sense of right, is out of the question," he wrote.

To his family he confessed genuine fear that the republican form of government might be doomed. "This new theory of representation will turn representatives into mere machines to record the public's will—swayed by every wind of ignorance and passion!"

Massachusetts Republicans would have returned John Quincy to Washington at once as their own representative. When he refused they continued to write him for advice. To them he was "an Atlas unshaken by the roaring blasts." Editorials in Salem and Boston pronounced him "the greatest ornament and the ablest member of the American Senate," prophesying that "if he persists in his dignified course he must one day attain to the highest station in our republic."

But John Quincy Adams was glad to be out of public life. At last he had leisure to enjoy his wife and growing family and to be near his aging parents. His renewed law practice thrived. Indeed, his fame brought more clients than he could handle, while several of his Harvard students were eager to serve their legal apprenticeship with him.

Early in 1809, he returned to Washington to plead a civil suit before the Supreme Court. He took Louisa with him to visit her family and witness the inauguration of James Madison as fourth President of the United States. Skinny "little Jemmy" appeared lost amidst the crowds that thronged the still unfinished Capitol. His short speech was delivered in a voice so low that it could hardly be heard.

"Mr. Madison cannot weigh more than an hundred pounds," John Quincy whispered to Louisa, "though he's not much shorter than I. I hope Mistress Dolley will hold his arm when he walks out in the March wind, else our new President may be whisked away!"

John Quincy escorted Louisa and her sisters, Nancy and eighteen-year-old Catherine, to the inaugural ball at Long's, the house kept by Stelle when he was senator. The crowded rooms were oppressively hot and John Quincy thought the entertainment poor. He paid his respects to the new President and his lady, and other old friends including Mr. Jefferson. Then he spent the rest of the evening trying to persuade the ladies to go home.

At breakfast two days later, a messenger delivered a note from Mr. Madison, requesting John Quincy to call on him at the President's House at his earliest convenience. Madison went straight to the point.

"I would like to nominate you as Minister Plenipotentiary to Russia," he told his friend. "Czar Alexander has frequently and strongly urged an interchange of ministers, and Mr. Jefferson and I have long wished to comply. Now the Senate is willing to make the appropriation. You know, John, that commercial relations with Russia are particularly important now, with our trade disrupted elsewhere—and with your experience, you might gain valuable advantages for us."

Taken by surprise, John Quincy had no ready answer. "I can see no immediate reason to refuse the appointment," he said hesitantly.

"I am truly sorry not to give you earlier notice," Mr. Madison apologized. "Let me send the nomination to the Senate while they are receptive to the idea. If you discover an insuperable obstacle, you may still decline."

From John Quincy's point of view there were many obstacles, each one of which might have stopped another man. A foreign post meant separation from his older sons who must remain in school, separation from his parents whom he might never again see in this life. It meant transporting Louisa from her comfortable home on Nassau Street to the Czar's lovely, but frigid northern capital—and with a baby less than two years old.

That night when he knelt to pray, as he did every night of his life, he remembered the agonizing indecision he had experienced before his first mission to Russia. Now he was in a position to do his country real service—and her need was surely as great.

"It is my clear duty to accept the post," he told Louisa at breakfast.

At the Court of the Czar

Winter gales whistled across the Gulf of Finland as the brig *Horace* battled the last reluctant miles of her journey to St. Petersburg. Although they had sailed from Boston early in August, the Adamses had been detained nearly a month in Denmark. There, in the harbor of Helsingör, they had discovered a fleet of American merchantmen interned for attempting to break through France's Continental blockade.

"Now see how Napoleon's embargo affects our overseas trade," John Quincy pointed out to the young men traveling with him. William Steuben Smith, Nabby's eldest son, accompanied him as private secretary, while two of his Harvard students, Alexander Everett and Francis Gray, had come at their own expense as apprentice diplomats.

The Americans had journeyed overland to Copenhagen to protest the internment of the vessels and crews to the French commissioner. The negotiations proved fruitless.

"Many English ships fly the American flag. As to the crews —American or English—" the French consul said with a shrug, "it is difficult to distinguish the one from the other, n'est-ce pas?"

John Quincy paced the *Horace*'s windswept deck during much of the three-week voyage through the Baltic Sea and up the Gulf of Finland, as if by the force of his will he could fend off the ice that soon would lock those waters tight until spring. In the cabin, Louisa and young Catherine huddled near a cozy reminder of home, the Franklin stove, installed for their comfort by the ship's owner, Mr. William Gray, young Francis' uncle. Thomas Nelson, the Negro valet, went about his chores with difficulty, since he had piled on every ounce of clothing he owned against the cold.

Only the toddler Charles Francis was completely happy. He ran about the cabins from dawn till dusk, while his nursemaid, Martha Godfrey, was kept warm chasing him. When the roll of the ship toppled him off his feet, he slid across the deck crowing with delight. The baby's antics diverted the whole party.

" 'Twas even later in October when I left St. Petersburg to join my father," John Quincy reminisced, catching his own son up in his arms. "Can it be twenty-six years ago!"

At dawn on October 23, John Quincy saw St. Petersburg appearing at the far end of the gulf. The multitude of domes that had impressed him on his earlier visit were the first objects to rise above the waterline. Fingers of red and gold from the rising sun were just touching the sleeping city to life as the *Horace* entered the broad mouth of the Neva River.

"But it's after nine o'clock!" exclaimed Louisa.

Her husband laughed. "And in summer, it stays light all night. Not bright sunlight," he reminisced, "but a pearly gray light that reveals every object, yet casts no shadow."

The brig slid past the jumble of dingy buildings on either side of the river, between ocean-going ships and river barges, to the quay where the American consul, Leverett Harris, was awaiting them. He had been expecting the ambassador's party for a month.

"I have an apartment for you in the Hotel de Londres," he told Ambassador Adams. "The rooms are indifferent, but the best to be found in the city."

John Quincy exclaimed excitedly at remembered landmarks as their carriage wound through the streets to the Nevskoi Prospekt where their hotel was located—Admiralty Square, the Winter Palace, and the gigantic statue of Peter the Great.

Having settled his family at the hotel, John Quincy instructed the consul to inform the Russian chancellor, Count Romanzoff, of his arrival. Two evenings later he attended a reception given by the count. The Ministers were requested to wear full dress. Out of the trunk came John Quincy's best suit and a long unused wig which Nelson powdered lovingly.

"The count received me cordially," he told his staff when he returned, "but Czar Alexander is confined with an inflammation of the legs, so I cannot meet with him for several days. One great problem here will be to keep up with their style of living." John Quincy looked down ruefully at his good black suit. "I was like a crow in a company of pheasants amongst the other foreign ministers, with their silks and velvets and gold braid!"

"But we cannot afford to renew our wardrobes, Uncle!" William Smith exclaimed.

"Each of us must buy one formal outfit in European style, for court functions," Ambassador Adams decided. "Otherwise they must take us as we are."

As in Berlin, they could not immediately find a house they could afford, so remained in lodgings that first winter. Louisa refused to appear at many social functions for want of a suitable gown. The dark sub-Arctic days and the silence of the snow-drenched city depressed her.

To John Quincy, the muted swish of the sleigh runners was soothing music, the snow a cleansing mantle, masking the sordid back street hovels. He wondered, though, how the "mougiks" or peasants survived the long cold winter. They moved through the silent streets like spectres in the weird half-light, carrying their pitiful fagots. He never saw them speak or show emotion. He never even saw a child laugh— nor, for that matter, cry.

The Adamses welcome was as warm as the climate was cold. John Quincy was liked and respected by the diplomatic corps, and in court circles, he was welcomed as an old friend. Louisa soon discovered that their simple way of life was considered charmingly democratic, and she was received cordially everywhere despite the comparative plainness of her dress.

The handsome young Czar went out of his way to be friendly, seeking out Louisa and her sister at their first court ball to dance the polonaise with them. John Quincy and the Czar shared a passion for early morning walks in all kinds of weather. They met often beside the Neva, and official courtesy soon blossomed into mutual respect and friendship.

John Quincy found the long dark afternoons perfect for writing and study. He began to learn Russian immediately, but as the winter wore on, he found his schedule turned upside down. Because there was no day, evening parties often lasted until four or five in the morning. The family seldom rose before nine—which was dawn—so John Quincy barely finished his Bible reading and his breakfast before the succession of visitors began. Between them and the state visits he must make, he had difficulty keeping up with the endless correspondence and reports required of an ambassador. Somehow, he still reserved several hours each day to play with and tutor his bright son, who spoke Russian, French and German as well as English before he ever entered school.

"I cannot continue to lead a life of such irregularity and dissipation," John Quincy often complained.

He was thankful for his three secretaries who helped with his official correspondence and made fair copies of reports and documents. The cold plus constant use made his right hand cramp painfully. He was endeavoring to train his left hand to write, but the results were nearly illegible. For quick notes he used a kind of shorthand, but only he could transcribe it.

If the life and his own domestic arrangements were not satisfactory, the prospects for his mission were better than he had dared hope. The Czar was a man of keen intelligence, with a reputation for independent and liberal views.

"We wish to increase our friendly intercourse with your country," he assured the American minister at their first meeting. "The United States is wise to remain aloof from Europe's unhappy disturbances. But England must be brought to terms in regard to her maritime pretensions, which are neither liberal nor just."

"The United States wishes to secure fair commerce to all nations in time of war," was John Quincy's careful reply.

The high chancellor, Count Romanzoff, was more specific. He admitted dissatisfaction with Napoleon's Continental blockade as a means to bring Britain to terms.

"We are greatly attached to a system of friendly commerce with the United States," he echoed the Czar's sentiments. "But, in this country, we are between the devil and the deep. The people are prejudiced in favor of England, out of habit and long-established custom. Yet her pretensions to exclusive rights upon the sea threaten the rights of all nations. It has become essential to support a rival."

John Quincy thought the count was arguing in favor of France's embargo. "The blockade does not impair Britain's commerce," he pointed out. "With European markets closed, neutrals are forced to trade with her exclusively, thus pouring into her lap the means of continuing the war!"

Count Romanzoff bowed his head in assent. "So it is in Russia's highest interest to support the United States, especially since, by their relative situation, the two powers could never be in any manner dangerous to each other."

Not long after the first meeting, Alexander sent a personal note to the King of Denmark advising him to release the American ships. Within the year, a ukase, or imperial decree, was issued declaring Russia's independence from Napoleon's Continental system. But the peace-loving nations of east and west could not long preserve neutrality in a world at war.

In January, 1811, John Quincy's two apprentices announced they must return home.

"The experience has been grand, sir," the young men assured him, "but we cannot afford to stay longer. Besides, letters from home warn that war with Britain may be inevitable. We should be there."

John Quincy sympathized with their financial plight. He had found a small house on the Moika, but even that modest household stretched his allowance. He had asked permission to return home himself, as soon as a treaty of commerce with Russia was concluded.

"President Madison has authorized me to leave when I wish," John Quincy told Alexander and Francis. "Our mission has been more successful than we knew. Secretary Monroe recently received a promise from Napoleon to lift the European blockade—at least to American commerce. Now that may damage Britain's trade enough to bring her to terms without war."

The valet, Nelson, went home with the young men, but John Quincy's nephew, William, remained to help him. The lad was courting Louisa's sister, Catherine, and a wedding appeared imminent.

In June, notice came that President Madison had appointed Ambassador Adams to the federal Supreme Court.

"We should hate to lose you," Count Romanzoff told John Quincy, "but I understand this is a great honor for you."

"An honor that I must refuse," John Quincy replied, "for now there is a tie that attaches me so strongly to this country that I cannot think of leaving. We are to be blessed with a new baby. I cannot subject Louisa to so hazardous a journey."

The whole court, even the Czar himself, and the entire diplomatic corps showed sincere interest in the small American that made her debut in the Russian capital on August 12, 1811. For Louisa and John Quincy the baby was a welcome daughter, Louisa Catherine. Yet loneliness for the sons at home grew with each passing year. John Quincy wrote them long letters concerning their education, urging especially that they read their Bibles regularly. He sent detailed instructions to Thomas, not even trusting him—now a learned judge of the Massachusetts Supreme Court—nor his ex-President father, to oversee his sons' studies. Ten-year-old George was his special concern. A nervous child, he was constantly at his books, yet his performance was erratic.

"Both his mother and his grandmother have babied him too much," John Quincy wrote Thomas. "Let him be encouraged in nothing delicate or effeminate. Let him mount on horseback . . . let him walk rather than ride in a carriage . . . let him skate this winter, swim next summer. In everything of this kind there is danger, but it is a world of danger in which we live, and I want my boys to be familiarized with its face, that they may be the better warned and guarded against it."

Danger was indeed closing in all around. Napoleon's armies were sweeping across Europe, engulfing nation after nation. Even Frederick of Prussia had been toppled from proud neutrality to unwilling alliance with the conqueror.

In mid-June, 1812, the French Army crossed the Russian frontier, on the very day that the United States Congress voted for war with Great Britain.

The thought of war was horrible to John Quincy—a new source of worry for his dear ones in New England. The terrors of his own boyhood haunted him like a troubled dream— the melting of the pewter spoons, the smoke and flames of Charlestown, the hourly dread of invasion from the sea. His aging parents must endure it all again, and now his sons.

War was not the only sorrow to come that year to the new home on the corner of Vosnesensky and Little Officer's Streets. The baby Louisa Catherine barely survived her first birthday.

". . . our only daughter . . ." the grief-stricken father cried out in rebellion against the cruel blow. "She was lovely as a seraph on earth." His was a long and silent struggle to bow humbly beneath the "chastening hand" of the stern God that ruled his life.

Within months came news of the death of Louisa's mother, then of her sister, Nancy—of unknown fevers.

While he tried to comfort Louisa, his own sister Nabby died. Forgetful of his own sorrow, he turned to comfort his nephew, Nabby's eldest son. The joy of William's recent marriage to Catherine was only a dim ray to illuminate the pall that hung over the lonely American family.

Their Russian friends were sympathetic and kind, but preoccupied with their own problems. The capital of war-torn Russia had become a gloomy city. John Quincy no longer glimpsed the towering figure of the Czar as he paced the quay by the Neva of a morning, for Alexander rode at the head of his troops. Napoleon's armies had penetrated Russia as far as Moscow, burning the city, but winter, and the barren steppes of that vast land nullified the victory. Rallying his forces, the Czar chased the tattered remnants of Napoleon's "unconquerable" army back to Paris. The bodies of men and horses lined the road of retreat, frozen where they dropped exhausted from hunger and cold.

Meanwhile, British armies in America resisted every attempt by the United States troops to invade Canada. Surprisingly, the infant U.S. Navy was winning unexpected victories against its seasoned adversary, both at sea and on the Great Lakes. Count Romanzoff teased the American ambassador about the contradiction.

"How does it happen that you are constantly beating the English at sea," he demanded, "where they beat the rest of the world? Yet on land, where you ought to be strongest, the English do as they please?"

"These times were reserved to keep the world in a state of wonder," John Quincy replied good-naturedly, "if only to prove there is something new under the sun."

10

★★★★★★★★★★★★★★★★★★★★   **10**   ★★★★★★★★★★★★★★★★★★★★

Waging Peace

Peace negotiations between Britain and the United States began before a battle was fought. In July, 1813, President Madison sent his Secretary of the Treasury, Albert Gallatin, and Senator James Bayard of Delaware to St. Petersburg to join John Quincy as peace envoys. It was not until April, 1814, that the British foreign office consented to have their commissioners meet the United States officials at Ghent, Belgium. John Quincy, Gallatin and Bayard were joined by Jonathan Russell, the youthful Swedish minister, and the fifth peace commissioner, Henry Clay.

England's foreign minister, Lord Castlereagh, had chosen his time well. Czar Alexander's rout of the French armies had brought peace to the continent. Napoleon was in exile, and Great Britain was free to turn all attention to the tiresome war across the Atlantic. The British press boasted that an army was sailing to take New Orleans and march up the rich Mississippi Valley to unite Canada with the Gulf of Mexico. In eastern Canada, another army was poised to strike south into New England where members of the Essex Junto were prepared to join them.

The first British demands were preposterous. They wanted exclusive military rights on the Great Lakes. They wished to establish an Indian buffer state between Canada and the United States, in territory already occupied by white settlers.

"They think we will break off the talks rather than yield," John Quincy surmised, "or at least send home for new instructions. Meanwhile their invasion may succeed or New England secede. We must make a counterattack."

"Peace is our object here," he told the British delegates. "We will discuss only problems arising out of the war—impressment, neutral rights, and indemnities for ship seizures."

The negotiations dragged on for weeks as the Americans sparred for time.

They heard with horror how the British had invaded the capital city and burned public buildings and the unfinished Capitol. Furious at this destruction they argued about their own stand, determined to fight on for years if necessary rather than consent to a bad treaty.

Then came word that the Americans had turned back an invading British fleet on Lake Champlain and chased the army back to Canada. And the army that had sacked Washington was stopped at Fort McHenry outside Baltimore and withdrew.

Before the armada bearing Wellington's veterans towards the Mississippi Delta ever reached its destination, the British delegates suddenly backed down from all offensive demands. On November 27, they announced to the surprised Americans that they would definitely abandon the Indian state and exclusive military possession of the Lakes. They would sign a peace on the basis of *status quo ante bellum*—the state before the war.

Mr. Madison had already instructed his peace delegates at

Ghent that impressment and neutral rights would no longer be an issue with the war over. John Quincy, with Clay and Gallatin, were to proceed to England to work out a commercial treaty. The controversial boundaries must be settled in a special convention.

On Christmas Eve, 1814, the treaty of peace was signed. Members of the two delegations celebrated together at a banquet marked by numerous toasts.

"I sincerely hope that the peace between our countries will be permanent," Lord Gambier announced with unaccustomed amiability.

"May it be the last treaty of peace between Great Britain and the United States," John Quincy concurred.

Later, in his chamber, John Quincy knelt to thank God "for the conclusion to which it has pleased Him to bring the negotiations for peace at this place."

Before John Quincy left Ghent, in February, 1815, notice arrived of his transfer from St. Petersburg to England as Minister Plenipotentiary to the Court of St. James. To return to Russia would consume too much time. Reluctantly, he wrote Louisa that she must close the house unaided and, with Charles Francis, travel across war-torn Europe to join him in Paris. There he enjoyed a month's vacation.

Early in March he became concerned about Louisa. Since she left St. Petersburg on February 12, he had received only one letter written during a week's stopover with friends in Berlin. Now there were rumors that Napoleon had escaped from the island of Elbe and was marching towards Paris while his scattered followers flocked to his standard. The society that had gathered around King Louis was quietly dissolving.

"Since the approach of Napoleon," John Quincy wrote his father, "vast numbers of foreigners, and many others, have left the city and taken flight in all directions. They have employed all the post horses on the road, so I am apprehensive my wife may have been detained for want of them."

Three endless days he waited, and when her mud-stained carriage finally drew up before the Hotel du Nord and she and Charles Francis tumbled wearily into his arms, the tale she babbled was astonishing. In forty days she had covered two thousand miles of winter roads, with only the week's respite in Berlin. She had dealt with thieving servants, replacing her Russian coachman in Germany for this reason. She had superintended the mending of broken wheels. Finally,, outside Paris, they had been mobbed by some of Napoleon's troops who thought they were Russian because of their carriage. The drunken men would have torn them to bits, she was certain, but for the intercession of an officer.

"This is an American lady," he shouted after examining her papers, "going to meet her husband in Paris."

"Vivent les Americains!" the soldiers shouted happily.

Louisa, instructed by the officer, leaned far out of the carriage, waved her handkerchief, and repeated, "Vive Napoleon!" as they inched down the road.

". . . and here we are." Louisa blinked wearily at the beloved face she had longed to see for so many months, then sank back on the huge feather bed and was asleep in minutes.

The reunited family spent six wonderful weeks in France's rejoicing capital, where the revolutionary tricolor flew once more. They glimpsed Napoleon once on the balcony of the Tuilleries, once in the palace chapel, but sensed his presence everywhere in the festive air. Their holiday ended with a ten-day visit with Lafayette at La Grange. In May, 1815, they sailed for England and a long-awaited reunion with George and John, already en route from New England to meet them.

Except for the Treaty of Commerce signed by Henry Clay, Albert Gallatin and John Quincy Adams in July, 1815, the two years in England were uneventful diplomatically. John Quincy found the foreign minister, Lord Castlereagh, cold.

". . . but not absolutely repulsive," he told Louisa.

The two brought many unsolved problems closer to settlement, especially the question of naval vessels on the Great Lakes.

After the peace was signed at Ghent, an increase of British fresh-water warships had set off a naval race on America's inland seas. Their presence caused several unpleasant incidents, any one of which might spark a new war.

"The British are at a definite disadvantage in any armament race on the Lakes," John Quincy pointed out to Lord Castlereagh. "We can easily double or triple any number of ships you send to such a remote outpost. The United States has no wish to conquer Canada now."

Though still suspicious, Lord Castlereagh admitted the absurdity of keeping armed ships parading the Lakes in peacetime. By 1817, the two diplomats had laid the groundwork for an accord to limit armed ships on the Lakes—the foundation for the eventual disarming of the whole border between Canada and the United States.

And by 1817, when the incoming President, James Monroe, appointed John Quincy to the office of Secretary of State that he himself was vacating, the Adamses were eager to go home.

11

★★★★★★★★★★★★★★★★★★★ **11** ★★★★★★★★★★★★★★★★★★★

Window on the West

After eight years of exile, the Adamses returned to a truly new America. No longer swayed by every shift in political thought across the sea, the country appeared to flex its growing muscles with adolescent pride as it turned all its thoughts and energy to the serious business of its own growth.

The steamers that plied the familiar waters of Long Island Sound were the most obvious innovation. John Quincy thought their black smoke was more offensively smelly than the gas lamps that illuminated some streets of London. But he booked passage to Boston on one, having learned they made the trip in half the time it took the sailing packets. He was as excited as his sons at the prospect of a ride on Mr. Fulton's marvelous invention.

On the morning of departure, John Quincy was writing in his chamber when George knocked on the door.

"It's almost seven o'clock, Papa," he called.

The steamboat was just pulling away from the wharf when their carriage rattled down Fulton Street. They had missed it by five minutes.

"The sailing packets never adhere to so strict a schedule,"

complained Louisa. She looked little and forlorn there on the wharf, surrounded by sleepy boys and mountains of baggage. They stood several minutes watching the steamer's stubby stern recede up the harbor, its side wheels churning noisily.

" 'Tis inexcusable of me to mistake the time," John Quincy mourned. He went at once to Crane's Wharf where he booked passage on the packet *Fame* preparing to sail for Providence that afternoon. From Providence they hired a coach to take them directly home.

John Quincy found his parents in perfect health, and the August days were bright with renewed friendships and the rediscovery of old haunts. With Thomas and the boys, he fished and hunted and swam off Black's Wharf. He and Louisa held court with the snowy-haired ex-President and his little lady outside the Quincy Meeting House on Sunday mornings. The pride of the elder Adamses in their son's accomplishments and prospects was boundless.

"People are already saying that you are worthy to preside over the Counsels of a Great Nation," his mother told him. "Would that I might live to see it."

There seemed no reason why she should not, for her bright-eyed interest belied the failing strength of her frail body.

"Take care of yourselves," the younger Adamses warned as they took a coach for Washington.

Once more they must leave their sons behind, George to enter Harvard, John and Charles to attend the Boston Latin School.

By alternating stage and steamboat, John Quincy and Louisa arrived at Washington on September 20, 1817. The city still resembled an unprosperous frontier town set down in a quagmire. The Capitol had been demolished by the

British and with it the congressional library that John Quincy had worked to establish when a senator.

"But I'm told that Mr. Jefferson has offered his own library when a new building is provided," John Quincy told Louisa as they bounced down Pennsylvania Avenue in a cloud of dust.

The hopeful rows of poplars that Jefferson had planted on either side of the avenue seemed to droop with shame amid the wasteland. The gravel spread to keep down the dust and fill the ruts was all washed away. Congress met in a temporary building called the "Brick Capitol" on the corner of Fifteenth Street, and the Department of State was housed in another brick building on Seventeenth Street, close to the executive mansion.

Here, on September 22, 1817, John Quincy took the oath as Secretary of State, assuming as he did a complexity of problems—some inherited from his predecessors, some brought with him from Europe. All were inherent in a dynamic nation that was already splitting the seams of its territorial waistcoat.

Since the nation's birth, a rising flood of emigrants from war-torn Europe and the impoverished British Isles had been flowing into the United States and westward across the Allegheny Mountains. By the time John Quincy assumed office, nearly two and a half million settlers were scrabbling for a living in the narrow strip of wilderness between the mountains and the Mississippi—as many as had populated the whole of the east coast colonies at the time of the revolution.

The pioneers wanted roads, canals, boats for the rivers— outlets for the products of their boundless energy. Most of all they wanted land. They fought the forest and the Indians and dreamed of an empire—a continental empire, united in freedom, that their new Secretary of State had long envisioned.

The most pressing problem when John Quincy became Secretary of State was that of Spanish Florida. The territory lay like a pistol pointed at the Mississippi, the continent's main artery. To control the river, President Jefferson had bought the Louisiana Territory and, John Quincy believed, West Florida.

Now it appeared, Spain claimed both East and West Florida, though for years she had been unable to rule either province adequately. Slaves were constantly escaping across the border from Georgia where they joined marauding Indians in harassing settlers to the north. Army divisions under General Andrew Jackson were frustrated in their war against the Seminoles because they could not pursue them into Spanish territory. Some thought the Spanish encouraged the Indians and supplied them with arms. Certainly no effort was made to stop the freebooters based on the offshore islands, who carried on piratical activities in the Atlantic and the Gulf of Mexico.

"I tried to buy the Floridas when I was Secretary of State," President Monroe told his successor. They conferred daily in his office at the "White" House, as the mansion had recently been named because of the quantities of white paint used to cover the scars of the British invasion. "Spain will let them go, but not for money." The big man shook his handsome head. "In exchange she wishes to extend her Texas territory east to the Mississippi."

Negotiations had reached this impasse when John Quincy began talks with the most practiced diplomat in Washington, Don Diego de Onis y Gonzales, whom he privately thought of as "Wily Don." The proud Spaniard was cold and overbearing. He had a supple, cunning mind, difficult to probe. Yet John Quincy admired his accomplished adversary—and pitied him as the representative of a weak and dying empire.

Spain's South American colonies were in rebellion. Venezuela had already declared independence, while the emerging republics of Chile and La Plata (Argentina) were clamoring for recognition. The situation complicated the Florida negotiation. The United States traded extensively with her neighbors to the south, and sympathy ran high for the revolutionaries.

"I am repeatedly insulted in my own home," Don Onis complained to Secretary Adams. "Windows are broken, and the lamps before the house have been smashed. Last night I found a dead fowl tied to the bell rope." The minister's dark face was crimson with outrage. "This is a gross insult to my sovereign! Does it not imply that he is of no more consequence than a dead hen?"

John Quincy could not help but sympathize with the Latin Americans' fierce desire for independence.

"Yet I seriously doubt that those people are suited, either by temperament or by training, for democratic self-government as we know it," he told the President. "Fortunately Don Onis believes the pranks are the work of South Americans now in the city. We must let nothing prejudice this country's strict neutrality during the Florida negotiations. I believe, if we can await the right moment, much more may be gained for this country than the Floridas."

Monroe's face wore a bewildered expression that was to become familiar to John Quincy in the next few years. "But there is a great deal of pressure from Congress to recognize the new countries," the President mused. "Speaker Henry Clay makes impassioned pleas to sway the House."

"Clay has mounted his South American great horse," John Quincy agreed. "He is hotheaded and often misguided, as I discovered during the conferences at Ghent, but he is devoted to the Union."

"Well, I have been insulted by foreign secretaries all over Europe," President Monroe admitted tiredly, "but this opposition from Congress and the constant bickering within the Cabinet itself, are very confusing."

Secretary of the Treasury William H. Crawford, a huge vital Virginian, avowedly coveted the Presidency, as did Henry Clay. They seized every opportunity to discredit Monroe—and his Secretary of State, most likely successor in that high office. William Wirt, the Attorney General, appeared to think more about "bread and meat for his children" than of affairs of state. John Quincy agreed that all their salaries were absurdly inadequate. His pitiful $3500 a year did not begin to cover his expenses, but after nearly a quarter of a century of public service he accepted this as a fact of life, in no way affecting the performance of his duty. In any case, there was now a bill before Congress to raise all their salaries.

"At least Mr. Calhoun appears to think for himself," he comforted his chief. "His judgments are sound, and he supports his opinions, too, with powerful eloquence."

This talent in the Secretary of War was one John Quincy admired particularly. Though persuasive in private audience, eloquent, even flowery, in prepared speeches, he remained nervous and constrained when speaking extemporaneously. He had just met John Calhoun, but liked the South Carolinian immediately, sensing in him a strength that seemed lacking in other members of the Cabinet.

During the protracted negotiations with Spain, unsettled

problems with England still vexed the Secretary of State, notably that of the boundary west from the Lake of the Woods, which for years he had fought to establish at the forty-ninth parallel. He instructed his successor at the Court of St. James, Richard Rush, to push an amicable settlement of all the questions unsettled at Ghent. British friendship would be important when the situation in Latin America demanded action.

To handle all these complex questions, John Quincy had the assistance of eight clerks. He personally must read and reply to every dispatch, a task with which his predecessor, James Monroe, had not kept pace. John Quincy found the Secretary's desk in a jumble when he assumed the office. Many important papers were missing entirely, including the translation of a recent treaty with Sweden.

"Our President is brilliant," John Quincy confided to Louisa, "but his mind works slowly, and apparently he is quite unmethodical."

The new Secretary immediately set the clerks to preparing a proper index system—one file for each American minister, one for consular correspondence, one for notes received from foreign ministers, and so forth. Gradually all state correspondence was put in order and brought up to date.

"Now, at least, we'll know where to find papers when we want them," he told his staff.

Putting the department in order had meant long hours for its head. The clerks left at 3:00 P.M., but their chief often stayed until dinner time, and sometimes the lamp in his office glowed into the night. On one occasion, the night watchman inadvertently locked the Secretary in the building, as he labored to catch up on routine business interrupted during the day by a constant stream of callers.

Besides the regular work of the department, its Secretary was required to perform a number of tiresome fringe duties. He affixed the great seal to all commissions signed by the President, and recorded them. He superintended the census, kept a register of federal officers, collected and tabulated the laws of the several states. Indian affairs were also a concern of his office.

In the midst of the mass of detail, John Quincy found time to formulate general standing instructions for newly appointed ministers and to reorganize the financial accounts. The department had always been in arrears with his own salary and expenses when he was a diplomat, he recalled. He also established a State Department library.

At the end of May, 1818, John Quincy bid adieu to Don Onis who was taking his family to summer in Bristol, Pennsylvania. His departure heralded restful days for the American Secretary—swimming in the Potomac on the bright, warm mornings; horseback riding beside the Tiber Creek with his friend Calhoun; and, later, a vacation with his parents in Quincy. Now he could make time for the essay on weights and measures that Congress had asked him to prepare, hoping to set a single standard throughout the states and territories.

But the Seminole Indians and General Jackson were not vacationing. Early in June, dispatches started flowing into Washington with news that Jackson had led his riflemen into Florida in pursuit of the marauding savages. The reports read like a swashbuckling serial. The lean Tennessean had seized the Spanish forts at St. Marks and Pensacola and chased the Indians far down the Gulf coast to their hideaway called Boleck's village. Two British subjects were captured with the Indians, tried and executed on the grounds that they had supplied them with arms and incited them to war.

An irate Don Onis rushed back to Washington to demand restitution, and members of the Administration were thrown into confusion.

"The general has committed war upon Spain which cannot be justified," Mr. Crawford declared nervously. "We must disavow his action!"

"He has certainly exceeded the instructions of my department," declared Mr. Calhoun, who actually appeared offended by Jackson's action.

"There might be cases which would justify General Jackson's measures," temporized Monroe.

John Quincy knew the President had long favored the acquisition of the Floridas at the proper time. Now he showed a lack of decision and a tendency to procrastinate that were disturbing. He had a high sense of duty, but adverse opinions and publicity unduly upset him.

The Secretary of State's cool New England twang silenced the buzzing. "General Jackson's orders were 'to adopt necessary measures' to end the troubles on the Florida border," he reminded his colleagues. "In my opinion, therefore, there has been no real violation of his instructions. His proceedings were justified by the necessities of the case, and by the misconduct of the Spanish officers who were derelict in their duty."

Day after day the deliberations continued as thin-lipped John Quincy defended General Jackson—alone.

"As to the Englishmen taken with the Indians," he told the President, "the British minister, Sir Charles Bagot, denies any perfidy on the part of his government. In other words, he repudiates the actions of the two renegades."

By mid-July John Quincy knew he was beaten. The strain

had caused his right hand, now palsied, to shake so that he could not report the discussions in writing.

"I still maintain that the government should assume full responsibility for General Jackson's action," he argued to the end. "If the question is dubious, it is better to err on the side of vigor than of weakness—on the side of our own officer, who has rendered the most eminent services to the nation, than on the side of our bitterest enemies."

The decision was to disavow Jackson and return the captured territory. Against John Quincy's strenuous objections, a paragraph was included declaring that the President thought Jackson had no constitutional power to take Pensacola without authorization from Congress.

The foray into Florida had demonstrated that the United States could easily take the territory by force, unless Spain received help to keep it. Despite the Administration's ambiguous position, John Quincy still felt that the moment he awaited was at hand, when more might be gained for his country than the Floridas. In August he took Louisa home for a well-earned rest on the shore of the cool Atlantic, but his mind's eye was fixed upon the blue waters of another ocean, a continent away. The United States needed a window on the west, overlooking the broad Pacific.

12

★★★★★★★★★★★★★★★★★★★★ **12** ★★★★★★★★★★★★★★★★★★★★

A New Declaration of Independence

On October 28, 1818, at the age of seventy-four, Abigail Adams died. John Quincy and Louisa had been home in Washington a little over a month when a letter from John confirmed the dread which they had felt since leaving Quincy.

To his bereaved father, whose mind at eighty-two was as keen as his body was wasted, John Quincy's heart reached out in mutual grief too great for words. For John Quincy himself, now in his fifty-first year, the loss of his mother was bitter. She had been his confidante and friend, with whom he could discuss the most involved problems of state. Her letters were a source of wisdom and inspiration. Her loving concern had been a bulwark for his political courage, now under attack from many quarters.

Some called Monroe's Administration the "era of good feelings." Ostensibly he governed without opposition. Since the Federalist party had ceased to exist as a national organization, the Republican was the only official party.

"But beneath the surface there is an interplay of passion

and intrigue such as I have never before witnessed," the Secretary of State confided to Alexander Everett during a visit from his former pupil. "Each man is a party unto himself, loyal only to himself. With the approaching election, half a dozen candidates have arisen to challenge Mr. Monroe —House Speaker Clay, Governor De Witt Clinton of New York, even the Secretary of the Treasury."

"There is a considerable party disposed to bring General Jackson forward as a candidate," young Everett said, "though the general says he's not such a 'damn fool' as to believe he's fit to be President."

John Quincy smiled at the blunt phrasing, so characteristic of the frontier soldier. "Still the partisans of each candidate find it to their interest to raise public opinion against the Administration—and, it seems, against me."

"Don't you think the newspapers should be informed of the opposition you face?" asked Alexander. "Will you do nothing to promote your own future election?"

"Nothing," John Quincy replied. "My business is to support the President, and to serve the public to the best of my abilities in the station assigned me. I have no time," he added wryly, "to intrigue for further advancement."

Spain's government had declared itself unsatisfied with the restoration of the Florida posts. The offending officer, General Jackson, must be censured and "suitably punished" or they would break off negotiations concerning the territory. At the same time, Don Onis was authorized to withdraw the Texas boundary demand from the Mississippi to the Sabine in return for the peaceful cession of the Floridas. President Monroe was inclined to accept the proposal.

"I believe a better boundary can be had," John Quincy told his chief. "A definite limit must be set to Spain's territory in North America. I wish to see the line drawn at the forty-first parallel straight through to the Pacific."

"Why that would transfer all Spain's Pacific coast territory north of California to the United States," exclaimed Monroe.

"Such a provision would better suit the nation," replied the Secretary of State.

"But how do you propose to defend Jackson?"

John Quincy had prepared a painstaking brief in defense of the general and of the Administration that drove home the real lesson of the Florida invasion. It stated boldly: "The President will neither inflict punishment nor pass censure upon General Jackson for conduct which is vindicated in every page of the law of nations—self-defense."

The United States demanded reparations to pay for the cost of Jackson's expedition, since, the paper maintained, the Spanish officers in Florida were guilty of misconduct. In not restraining the savages under their jurisdiction, they had

> acted in defiance and violation of the engagements of Spain with the United States.
>
> . . . Spain must immediately make her election, either to place a force in Florida adequate to the protection of her territory and to the fulfillment of her engagements, or cede to the United States a province of which she retains nothing but nominal possession, which is, in fact, a derelict, open to the occupancy of every enemy. . . .

The note carried all before it. Overwhelming majorities in the House voted down the motion to censure General Jackson. In Britain, Lord Castlereagh advised Spain to yield Florida in the interest of world peace. The point was emphasized by the conclusion of an Anglo-American Convention in the midst of the furor. The terms marked a sturdy advancement of friendly relations between England and her offspring.

New England fishermen secured "forever" rights to the best inshore fisheries of British America. In the northwest the boundaries were left "free and open for a term of ten years to the vessels, citizens and subjects of the two powers." To the Rockies, the boundary was fixed at the forty-ninth parallel, a triumph for the United States, and for the patient motives of John Quincy Adams.

Spain was left with little choice but to come to terms with the United States. Don Onis fought a valiant rear-guard action to retain as much as possible of his country's dissolving empire.

"You are harder to deal with than the President," he conceded gracefully when he met the American Secretary to exchange copies of the treaty.

It was February 22, 1819—George Washington's birthday anniversary. John Quincy thought the treaty was a fitting tribute to the founder of the country.

The King of Spain ceded to the United States "all territories which belong to him situated to the eastward of the Mississippi and known by the name of East and West Florida." Texas' eastern boundary was fixed at the Sabine, but north of the forty-second parallel, all the way to the Pacific, the territories of New Spain were transferred to the United States. It was truly a "transcontinental" treaty.

Ferdinand, King of Spain, was far from pleased with the terms of the treaty and delayed ratification for two years. Meanwhile the United States was suffering a serious financial depression that pushed the matter into the background. Distress and rumblings of discontent spread across the nation as farm prices toppled and merchants failed.

That same year, the application of the Missouri Territory

for statehood exposed the "abscess on the national body," as John Quincy once called slavery.

"Slavery is already well established in Missouri as it was part of the original Louisiana Purchase," he explained to his sons, who were home for the holiday. "But to admit the territory as a slave state would upset the sectional balance."

Since the admission of Alabama earlier that year, the balance stood at eleven free and eleven slave states. The Ohio River formed the natural boundary between slavery and freedom in the West. Above the river, in the "Northwest Territory," slavery had been prohibited "forever" by the Ordinance of 1787. But it was not so much the northern location of the would-be state, nor was it entirely humanitarian or religious abhorrence to the South's "peculiar" institution, that prompted an all-out battle by northern antislavery blocs against her admission as a slave state.

"Where slavery exists," John Quincy explained to the young people, "a slaveowner is allowed three votes for every five slaves he owns."

"But that's not fair," exclaimed George. "Allowing representations for slaves must give southern states greater influence in the legislature than their size warrants."

John Quincy liked the way his son's mind made quick, logical judgments. Yet the nineteen-year-old remained nervous and moody and was erratic in scholastic performance. Lately though, he had shown a romantic interest in his orphaned cousin, sixteen-year-old Mary Catherine Hellen, who had lived with her Aunt and Uncle Adams since their return to Washington.

In an effort to reach a compromise, Representative James Talmadge of New York suggested an amendment to the Missouri bill which would prohibit further introduction of slaves into Missouri and provide for the gradual emancipation of those already there.

"The federal government has no right to interfere with domestic institutions," cried southern politicians, "nor with a citizen's free enjoyment of his property!"

The bitter controversy lasted two years, during which John Quincy attended the debates as often as his own affairs would permit.

"Slaveholders cannot even discuss this question without being seized with cramps," he exploded at home.

Henry Clay took a pessimistic view, predicting that in five years the Union would be divided into three confederacies. John Calhoun was more optimistic.

"I do not believe the slave question will produce a dissolution of the Union as you fear, John," he told Secretary Adams as they walked home from the Hill together on a February evening, "but if it should, the South would be necessarily compelled to form an alliance with Great Britain. The North should be cut off from its natural outlet upon the ocean, and must fall back upon its rocks to starve."

John Quincy was shocked that a man whom he called friend could even consider such an eventuality.

"The question has betrayed the secret of men's souls," he told Edward Everett, Alexander's brother. Now a Unitarian minister and professor of Greek at Harvard, young Everett was in Washington to deliver a series of lectures.

John Quincy paced before the fire in the study of his recently purchased home on F Street at Thirteenth. "I have always thought Calhoun was a man of sound judgment, independent of the rest. Now all his powerful oratory is thrown on the slavish side of this question, when the mass of plain sense is on the side of freedom and humanity!

"What, I ask you, could be more false and heartless than this doctrine which makes the first and holiest rights of man depend upon the color of the skin?" he cried, shaking his finger at his sympathetic visitor as if he were a southern congressman. "I bid you, visit the slave marts while you are here. Witness the bartering of human flesh in the very shadow of freedom's capital!"

"Too bad you are not in Congress, sir," Edward Everett smiled. "The cause of freedom needs men with your logic and eloquence."

Eloquence? thought John Quincy. Yes. On this question he could speak endlessly without restraint.

"If a man could arise," he mused aloud, "with a genius capable of comprehending, a heart capable of supporting, and an utterance capable of communicating those eternal truths that belong to this question; such a man would perform the duties of an angel upon earth! But the Union may break apart before this foul stain is eradicated!"

While the controversy raged, Maine, a former district of Massachusetts, applied for statehood. Speaker Clay pushed the acceptance of both states, engineering the "compromise" that re-established the sectional balance.

"So slavery is perpetuated in Missouri," said John Quincy, "and, for the present, the issue is laid asleep. But I fear this contest is but the title page to a great tragic volume."

Though torn internally, the country was expanding in other ways. Many eyes were turning to the Northwest. New Englanders engaged in whaling operations needed bases on the Pacific, and fur traders, such as John Jacob Astor, were establishing trading posts.

British Minister Stratford Canning, who had replaced Sir Charles Bagot, protested to John Quincy about rumors that

Astor's settlement at the mouth of the Columbia River was to be enlarged.

"Such an increase violates the Convention of 1818," claimed Canning.

Without replying, John Quincy searched his bookcase for the volume of laws of the United States which contained the convention. When he found it, he quoted the section that the boundaries were to be left "free and open."

"Now, sir," said John Quincy, "if you feel my government has violated this article, please make your charge in writing."

"Do you not know that we have a claim to the mouth of the Columbia?" Canning cried, infuriated.

"I do not know what you claim," the American Secretary replied smoothly, "but when you speak of treaties, I must have it in writing. You claim India, you claim Africa . . ."

"Perhaps a piece of the moon?" was the sarcastic rejoinder.

"No," replied John Quincy, "I have not heard that you claim exclusively any part of the moon; but there is no spot on this habitable globe that I could affirm you do not claim. There is none, however, to which you have less right than to the mouth of the Columbia River."

"And how far would you consider this exclusion of right to extend?" asked the surprised British minister.

"To all the shores of the South Sea," the American Secretary replied.

"Suppose Great Britain should undertake to make a settlement there," asked Canning, "would you object?"

"I have no doubt we should," John Quincy replied.

Soon after Monroe's second inaugural, John Quincy was confronted by another adversary in the Northwest. Russia owned Alaska and Russian fur traders freely ranged the coast south to California. In 1821, Czar Alexander ordered all foreign ships to keep 100 miles away from the Northwest coast south to the fifty-first parallel. The ukase (imperial order) interfered with American whalers and traders as well as implying a larger territorial claim than existed. The friendly Russians answered John Quincy's protest with an offer to negotiate.

In 1822, President Monroe determined to recognize five new South American nations—La Plata (Argentina), Chile, Peru, Colombia and Mexico. Congress voted appropriations to send missions to the new governments despite the threat of Spain and her allies—France, Russia and Prussia—that they would send a vast armada to recover the lost colonies.

In the matter of Cuba's application for statehood that September, John Quincy counseled the President to be less bold.

"Say that the Executive of the United States is not competent to promise them admission as a state in the Union," he advised Monroe. "It is one thing to recognize an existing government, but the taking of Cuba, even by request, could be construed as aggression. Britain would surely fight to prevent it; yet, if the island is left in Spain's hands, it will doubtless fall to us eventually as did the Floridas."

When Baron Tuyl arrived from Russia in the spring of 1823 to discuss the question of the northwest coast, John Quincy voiced to him the same evolving principle that he had suggested to the British minister the year before.

"The United States will contest the right of Russia to any further territorial establishment on this continent. We assume distinctly that the American continents are no longer subjects for any new European colonial establishments."

The plural of the word continent was used intentionally. Having recognized the South American nations, the United States would defend their liberty as she would her own.

That autumn of 1823, Great Britain suggested a joint declaration to the world that they would oppose any European movement in Latin America. Backed by the approval of two former Presidents, James Madison and Thomas Jefferson, as well as of most of his Cabinet, the President was inclined to sign the joint statement. The Secretary of State alone objected.

"Mr. Canning's statement includes a pledge that neither the United States nor Great Britain will seek further territory in this hemisphere," he pointed out to the Cabinet. "Certainly we have no intention of seizing either Texas or Cuba, for instance, but the inhabitants of either territory might, at some future date, wish to exercise their primitive rights and solicit union with us. We should keep ourselves free to act as emergencies arise.

"It would be more candid, as well as more dignified, to avow our principles explicitly, rather than as a cockboat in the wake of the British man-of-war."

President Monroe had no desire to appear subordinate to Britain, and members of the Cabinet fell into line. The Secretary of State was instructed to make a draft of the minutes of the meetings for a public message on the subject.

"The Russian note might be the basis for such a message," Monroe suggested, "that the American continents are henceforth not to be considered as subjects for future colonization."

"We should make it clear, at the same time, that we will not interfere in European affairs or with existing colonies, nor attempt to spread our principles abroad," added John Quincy.

The statements were incorporated into President Monroe's message to Congress on December 2, 1823. Though the decision to defend the independence of South America might mean war, the statements were received favorably both in Congress and in the press. Speaker Clay thought the pronouncement long overdue: ". . . even if it means war against all Europe, including England," he declared. The "Warhawk" of 1812 had mellowed very little, John Quincy thought.

Rumors that Spain and her allies might invade South America disturbed the President.

"Britain is incensed and rumors from Europe announce that an army of twelve thousand Spaniards is ready to embark immediately to subdue South America," John Quincy heard a reporter from the *National Intelligencer* tell Mr. Monroe.

"On another page the disbanding of the Spanish Army is announced," Secretary Adams assured the President.

At home, with his stockinged feet propped on the fireguard, he confided to Louisa, "We have made a new Declaration of Independence, my dear. A hemispheric declaration! Let's hope we'll not have to fight for this one."

"You look very tired, John," Louisa said with wifely concern. The handsome face she had first loved was creased with care, the full lips pressed into a harsh line. "You work too hard, and worry too much."

John Quincy smiled at her fondly. In the six years he had been Secretary of State, his country had grown from a hodgepodge of bickering states to a continental power to be reckoned with in world politics. To assert their new position they had been forced to march to the brink of war.

"I am tired," John Quincy confessed. "Very, very tired."

13

★★★★★★★★★★★★★★★★★★★★ **13** ★★★★★★★★★★★★★★★★★★★★

President Under Fire

During the first week of January, 1824, the Adams' house on F Street rang with the laughter of the young people. George and John, Charles Francis on vacation from Harvard, and their cousins, Mary Catherine and young Abigail, daughter of John Quincy's brother Charles, were preparing the spacious rooms for a reception honoring General Jackson—now Senator Jackson—on the tenth anniversary of his victory over the British at New Orleans.

The ballroom was festooned with garlands of flowers and the furniture moved aside in all the downstairs rooms, for over one thousand guests were expected. For days, Washington government and diplomatic circles had talked of little else than this "affair" of the season. The editor of the *National Journal* was even moved to poetry.

> Wend ye to the ball tonight?
> All are gone to Mistress Adams'.
> Belles and matrons, maids and madams,
> All are gone to Mistress Adams'.

Louisa, at forty-eight, was lovely as ever in a dignified steel-gray gown with cut-steel ornamentation, as she graciously received her guests. John Quincy, who usually abhorred large formal affairs, was an affable, even jolly host. In that fashionable assemblage, he was the most simply dressed of all the men. Even the uniform of the guest of honor paled to insignificance beside the more colorful uniforms of foreign attachés, and the vivid Cossack trousers and Hessian-type boots that were favored by young men of fashion.

Diplomats, congressmen and Cabinet members danced with their ladies until dawn, all antagonisms buried for the moment over the punch bowls. But the rivalries that had roiled beneath the calm surface of James Monroe's Administration, boiled up in that election year in a tidal wave of bitterness.

John Quincy Adams, as Secretary of State, was "heir apparent" to the Presidency. He was the nominee of the northeastern states. Yet he was a man without a party. Nothing in his training or nature fitted him for the peculiar dealings of the politician. His office left him no time, as he had told Alexander Everett, to intrigue for advancement, even had he been so inclined.

Opposed to him were the wily and unscrupulous William Crawford, who campaigned to the bitter end despite a paralytic stroke, and the ambitious and popular House Speaker, Henry Clay. A surge of hero worship swept General Jackson ahead of all of them to win the majority vote that fall, but not a decisive majority over John Quincy. The House of Representatives must decide the issue.

"I am surprised that a silent animal like myself could give the hero of New Orleans so close a race," John Quincy confessed to Daniel Webster, senator from Massachusetts, who was campaigning for him amongst the legislators. "Well, I believe General Jackson will make a good executive."

Henry Clay did not agree. "I have never felt warmly

towards that Massachusetts Puritan," he said of John Quincy to a Kentucky colleague. "On the other hand, shooting a few Indians does not qualify a man for the Presidency. No, I shall throw my votes to John Quincy Adams. He is the best-qualified man for the job."

Clay's influence in the West and South was no longer equal to Jackson's, but it was enough to tip the scale. Jackson advocates were furious, crying that the two had made a corrupt bargain—that Clay had sold his support to Adams. Jacksonian newspapers had poured out a continual stream of slander throughout the campaign, but now their barbs became so deadly that Andrew Jackson himself became convinced that his friend and defender had plotted to defeat him.

"So the bitterness must follow me even into the Executive Mansion," moaned the President-elect.

Long before dawn of Inauguration Day, March 4, 1825, firelight flickered in the second-floor library of the Adams' house. John Quincy stood at the window staring down the hill toward Pennsylvania Avenue. Mr. Jefferson's poplars swayed in the gray light, like wraiths treading a stately measure. Shivering, the President-elect turned to kneel close to the comforting blaze and pray. His head was heavy from lack of sleep. His body ached with tension built up over the months of the campaign. This day should mark the culmination of nearly thirty years of service to his country, yet his victory was like ashes. For the call to the highest office in the land had been only a grudging whisper.

At 11:30 A.M., Samuel Southard, Secretary of the Navy, and William Wirt, Attorney General, came for John Quincy. As they escorted him to a waiting carriage, President Monroe called a cheery "good morning" from his own carriage. In a third conveyance rode Louisa with their sons and the two nieces.

John Quincy's spirit lifted as the cavalcade trotted into Pennsylvania Avenue. A militia band struck up "Yankee Doodle," as several companies snapped to attention to escort the carriages to the Capitol. Cheering citizens lined the way and ran along behind. John Quincy smiled and waved to them, feeling at last the glow of victory. After all, nearly half the nation had voted for him.

The Presidential party went directly to the Senate chamber where John Calhoun had already been sworn in as Vice-President. The senators, with the judges of the Supreme Court like nine brooding muses in their black robes, escorted the President-elect to the House chamber.

In his plain dark suit, John Quincy Adams was the picture of an executive as he climbed the speaker's platform to deliver his inaugural address. Though a short, heavy man, his patrician head set on a powerful neck was reminiscent of a bust of a Roman senator. The lines of care, the tense, thin lips, even the baldness which gave his brow an endless sweep, seemed in keeping with the eminence he had attained. His broad swimmer's shoulders, slightly hunched from years of bending to a writing desk, gave him a combative look.

"I appear, my fellow citizens, in your presence and in that of Heaven to bind myself by the solemnities of religious obligation to the faithful performance of the duties allotted to me," he commenced.

He spoke with pride of the thirty-six years of the nation's growth in which he had served every Administration.

Chief Justice John Marshall administered the oath of office. Andrew Jackson was the first to step forward and shake the new President's hand.

On March 5, John Quincy sent his new Cabinet appointments to the Senate. They were few.

"Cabinet posts as well as civil service appointments should be based on merit and experience rather than political favoritism," he explained when Mr. Monroe questioned his retaining in office men who had campaigned against him. "I am determinated to renominate every person against whom there is no complaint which would warrant his removal."

To the treasury post, vacated by William Crawford, John Quincy named Richard Rush, who, for the past six years, had ably served as minister to England. Governor James Barbour of Virginia replaced John Calhoun in the War Department. To take his own vacated office in State, John Quincy named Henry Clay.

"Under the circumstances, that appointment is unwise, John," warned James Monroe.

"I consider it his due," John Quincy insisted. "Anyone who questions Mr. Clay's qualifications need only look about amongst statesmen and legislators. What man has more preeminent talents? Where is there a more ardent patriot?"

The appointment convinced Andrew Jackson that the two men had, indeed, made a corrupt bargain, and turned the Indian fighter into an implacable enemy of the Administration. Jackson could not know that the man who had nosed him out of the Presidency remained his stanch admirer and supporter. So little regard did John Quincy have for political expediency, he even considered naming his rival Secretary of War.

With Congress recessed, the first summer of the Presidency passed quietly. John Quincy continued to rise early to read his Bible, to walk or ride horseback, or to swim with John, now his secretary; Charles Francis, who had graduated from

Harvard that June; and Antoine, the Belgian ex-soldier who had been his valet and friend since Ghent.

The new President made frequent visits to the White House dairy, housed in a low shed extending from one side of the mansion, and he personally supervised the care of the eight fine carriage horses stabled in a similar low wing on the other side.

"Busy as you are, Father," John remonstrated, "surely you could leave the milking of the cows to the stable boys!"

"The cows and the horses are better company than most of the callers that plague my every waking hour!"

Many of the President's visitors were cranks and office seekers. They consumed so much of his day that the reading and signing of state papers kept him busy into the night, a routine he had established as Secretary of State. Now, however, he did set aside an hour each evening to play billiards or chess with his sons or with favored guests.

The August days were brightened by the presence of the dapper, white-haired Marquis de Lafayette who, with his son George Washington, had been making a triumphal tour of the United States.

When John Quincy went home in September, he found that his father had become so blind and feeble he could not walk across a room unaided. Yet he discussed the program his son planned to put before Congress in December with animation.

"Not that you'll get one-third what you ask for internal improvements," he warned, "but even that would be more than all your predecessors put together."

"I cannot see why anyone would take issue with this program," mused John Quincy, "since its sole aim is the broadening and strengthening of the Union."

The ninety-year-old ex-President closed his eyes and let his ancient head drop upon his chest, as his mind receded to his own stormy Administration. He placed a gnarled hand on his son's sleeve.

"The presidential chair is no bed of roses, my boy," he said finally.

During that peaceful summer, storm clouds were already forming. The day after his inauguration, John Quincy had signed the Treaty of Indian Springs, negotiated between the state of Georgia and "the Chiefs of the Creek nation, in council assembled."

˙ The Creek and Cherokee tribes of Georgia were the most civilized of all North American Indians. They were farmers and shepherds to whom their land was precious. By a treaty in 1791, the United States had guaranteed to them land they occupied in what had since become western Georgia. As the white population increased, the newcomers began to covet the Indian lands.

As Secretary of State, John Quincy had watched the growing struggle. The refusal of the Cherokees to move caused grave concern, so he was relieved that the Creeks, at least, had settled the question peaceably by treaty.

On December 5, 1825, the Nineteenth Congress assembled. The following day, President Adams submitted to them his program. It was simple and robust. Individual liberty had been secured, at least for white citizens. Protection of property and improvement of the land was his concern. He suggested "laws promoting the improvement of agriculture, commerce, and manufactures, the cultivation of the mechanic and the elegant arts, the advancement of literature, and the progress of the sciences, ornamental and profound."

Long ago in Russia, John Quincy had dreamed of a continental republic, peopled by a mighty race of free men, marching under one flag, speaking one language, a power such as man had never before witnessed on earth. The first necessity for such a nation was union, and a strong national government. John Quincy believed the Constitution gave the federal government broad powers to protect its citizens and their property. His plan went far beyond Clay's "American Plan" or that of any of his predecessors.

Besides a vast network of roads and canals to unite all sections of the country more closely, he wished to control the sale of western lands to pay for the improvements that would enhance their value—and to reduce the national debt.

The recent depression had pointed up the evil of wildcat land speculation and also the need for a sound national banking system and uniform bankruptcy laws.

He asked for a new Department of the Interior devoted solely to the affairs of a burgeoning population. He asked for a humane policy of Indian removal, suggesting they be transferred west of the Mississippi and educated for eventual citizenship.

He recommended West Point to the patronage of the nation. The army was made up of uncoordinated groups of state militia. Officers were needed to train a national army for common defense. He envisioned, too, officers equipped to lead a new corps of engineers to make scientific expeditions, especially into the unexplored regions of the Far West, and to survey routes for the new roads and canals.

By the same token, John Quincy wished to strengthen the peacetime navy and establish an academy similar to West Point to train its officers.

"It is a dangerous illusion to believe that a commerce so extensive and so rich as ours could exist and be pursued in safety without the continual support of a military marine."

To guard that commerce and foster native industry, he recommended a cautious tariff.

John Quincy even touched on the dredging of harbors and rivers, and the need for lighthouses along the coast.

But President Adams did not stop with physical improvements. To enjoy liberty, a people must be enlightened, and John Quincy conceived it the duty of the President to point the way.

"The first condition for improvement of men is knowledge," he said in asking for a national university and a national astronomical observatory for the advancement of science. "The United States has not a single observatory! New discoveries must be received secondhand from Europe. If we reflect upon the discoveries which in the last four centuries have been made in the physical constitution of the universe by means of observatories, shall we doubt their usefulness?"

In closing his inaugural speech, John Quincy warned the legislators not to

> hide in the earth the talent committed to our charge. . . . The nation blessed with the largest portion of liberty must in proportion to its numbers be the most powerful nation upon earth. . . . While foreign nations less blessed with that freedom which is power than ourselves are advancing with gigantic strides in the career of public improvement, were we to slumber in indolence or fold up our arms and proclaim to the world that we are palsied by the will of our constituents, would it not be to cast away the bounties of Providence and doom ourselves to perpetual inferiority?

Speaker John Taylor of New York called at the Executive Mansion to congratulate the President on his program. So did Daniel Webster and Edward Everett, now senators from

Massachusetts. Robert Livingston of Louisiana vowed he agreed with the Adams message in every part. He was alone among southern congressmen.

Canny Daniel Webster warned that many would fight the allotting of so much power to the federal government.

"I still think you should have left out the university and perhaps the observatory," Henry Clay asserted. "They have little chance of success."

James Barbour, his new Secretary of War, was nervous about the whole section on internal improvements.

"It's a good thing you're stubborn, John," Clay said finally, "else we would have stripped you of your draft completely."

Henry Clay's respect for his chief had turned to affection. During that summer the Secretary of State had lost two daughters to yellow fever, and John Quincy had shown a warm sympathy that the Kentuckian had never believed existed behind the cold New England manner. In his grief, Henry Clay had been allowed to glimpse the long-hidden void in John Quincy's own heart caused by the loss of his only daughter. The inevitable clashes between the two strong personalities were tempered now by friendship and mutual understanding.

"During Cabinet discussions of my message," John Quincy told the senators laughingly, "I was like the man with two wives in Addison's *Spectator*. The one plucked out his white hairs, the other his black, until none were left."

In Congress, the nucleus of a new party had already formed, whose aim was to pluck apart President Adams' program until there was nothing left. Made up of partisans of Jackson, Calhoun and Crawford, they called themselves Democratic Republicans, as opposed to the Adamsites, or National Republicans. Party members came from the South where states' rights were jealously guarded. The "liberty which is power" spoken of by President Adams was feared in the South as a potential danger to their "peculiar" institution of slavery.

Democrats came, too, from the West where the pioneers wanted land but as little government as possible. They were joined by many northern Republicans, who were alarmed by the President's broad construction of governmental powers, so far removed from the looser interpretation of Jefferson.

Few politicians wanted an enlightened populace. The untutored were more easily swayed. Newspapers across the land lampooned John Quincy's "lighthouses in the skies," as he had unfortunately called observatories, and painted a lurid picture of the proposed national university where unsuspecting youth would surely be imbued with dangerous ideas.

"Be the Administration purer than the angels," vowed leaders of the "democracy," "it shall be overthrown."

The opposition showed itself immediately in the debate over participation in an international conference at Panama called by the Venezuelan liberator, Simon Bolivar. The President and Secretary of State Clay urged cooperation with the new South American republics and two delegates were appointed. Southern legislators, who hated the idea that white Americans must mingle with colored delegates from Haiti, delayed confirmation of the executive appointments until the mission became futile. One American died en route to Panama, while the second arrived after the conference was over.

The voice of opposition grew shriller when the Administration asked for federal troops to protect the lands of the Creeks and the Cherokees from invasion by Georgians. Secretary Barbour's investigators had discovered that the Indian Springs' Treaty had been obtained from a rump group of lesser Creek tribes. For a bonus of $400,000 a chieftain had sold his brethren out.

Governor Troup defied the President's order to stay off Indian lands until a new treaty could be negotiated. "Georgia is sovereign on her own soil," he insisted and sent his surveyors in with state militia to protect them. "We will fight federal troops if they appear."

Congress feared that a battle between the federal government and a state would surely destroy the Union. In the end, the Indians were forced to cede their lands and John Quincy's attempt to protect their rights only made him more unpopular —in the South where he was condemned for encroaching on state rights, in the West where getting rid of the Indians was a prime concern.

"The lines of the political combination against us is clear," John Quincy told his Cabinet.

It was a combination that would eventually split the Union apart—but not while John Quincy Adams had breath in his body.

14

Old Soldiers Never Die

Thomas Jefferson died at his home in Monticello, Virginia, on July 4, 1826, at ten minutes past one in the afternoon. At 5:00 P.M. the same day, John Adams breathed his last in Quincy, Massachusetts. It was the fiftieth anniversary of the signing of the Declaration of Independence.

"Grandfather's last thoughts were of Mr. Jefferson," George told his father and brothers when they arrived from Washington.

"Despite their differences, father loved Mr. Jefferson," John Quincy affirmed. "They grew close again at the end through their letters, as they had been in the beginning when together they conceived our immortal Declaration. That these two have embarked together on their last journey seems to me a mark of Divine favor for which we should be humbly grateful."

That summer, while the nation mourned the loss of the two founding fathers, their President endured his private grief alone in the mansion where his parents had lived for nearly forty years. Here John Quincy had spent many of the happiest days of his life, close to the two people whom he had loved and admired more than any other human beings. With them gone, the gracious rooms seemed to have lost their charm, yet he could not face the thought of abandoning the house.

"Within two or three years I shall need a place of retirement," he decided, "and this will be a safe and pleasant retreat . . . though I cannot realize what retirement will be like," he confessed to George, who had just begun a promising career in the Massachusetts legislature. "Still, it cannot be worse than this perpetual motion and the crazing cares of public life. Sometimes I feel ready for the churchyard myself."

Within the White House life was as peaceful as the political scene was stormy. Visitors often discovered the President working in his tree nursery, his bald head shaded by a battered straw hat. He experimented with exotic types from South America and Europe—Spanish cork-oak, black walnut and almond—while nearby the First Lady might be seen expertly winding silk from the cocoons of the silkworms she raised.

At dawn every fine summer morning, the rotund Chief Executive and his brawny dark-haired valet walked across the south grounds to Tiber Creek which flowed across Fifteenth Street into the Potomac. John, and sometimes Charles Francis, would run ahead to prepare the old rowboat kept docked at the bottom of Seventeenth Street. The boys would swim across the inlet to the rise of ground that formed the estuary, but John Quincy, in his sixtieth year, found the long swim tired him excessively. Antoine rowed him to the islet. There on a rock beneath a sycamore tree, the President would peel off his clothes and dive in "au naturel," with Antoine always close beside him.

During the first year of his Presidency, a sudden gust of

wind upset their boat halfway across the creek. With the sleeves of his shirt dragging at his arms, John Quincy had barely made the shore half a mile distant. After that, he almost gave up swimming, but Antoine and John persuaded him not to abandon an activity that gave him so much pleasure. Between them they agreed that he should never swim alone, or more than a few minutes at a time.

Louisa's health grew worse in the White House, which excused John Quincy from attending the large formal affairs that he had always detested. At intimate dinners, he talked with sparkle and wit. Louisa remained a superb hostess, but, as criticism of her husband mounted with the approaching campaign, she began ot resent the need to entertain political opponents.

"They snoop about to find something to criticize," she complained.

Indeed, some newspapers accused the President of running a "gambling hall" in the White House game room when a reporter spied the billiard table John Quincy had purchased. The absurdity of the accusation was lost on ignorant frontiersmen. Others charged that Louisa was extravagant because of the exquisite French pieces with which she had furnished the barren East Room. The fact that they came from her own home was ignored.

"Why is it their business, since we have not used their money for these few niceties!" Louisa wept.

"You will not have to bear the slanders much longer, my dear," John Quincy assured her. "The Democrats are bound to unseat me—and doubtless will in the next election."

John Quincy already realized that his broad program was too progressive for the times. Yet his Administration, with the aid of a strong and loyal minority in Congress, was chalking up an unprecedented record of peace abroad and advancement at home. Commercial treaties were negotiated with the major nations of Europe and Central America, while at home, several satisfactory Indian treaties were concluded. Through careful handling, the national debt was steadily reduced.

The movement west had become an avalanche. With the settlers went the new Army Engineers to survey sites for turnpikes and canals. The National Road was extended west to Zanesville, and its route surveyed to Jefferson City, capital of the new state of Missouri. Steamboats on the dredged and widened rivers of the West linked the far-flung growing settlements.

Along the eastern coast, harbor channels were deepened and charted. An increasing number of lighthouses projected a bright welcome into the dark Atlantic. A bill was passed authorizing the maintenance and improvement of the navy, though stripped of half its worth, John Quincy thought, by the exclusion of an academy to train its officers.

In 1826, a group of New Yorkers obtained a charter for the Mohawk and Hudson Railroad, and in 1828, Charles Carroll, last surviving signer of the Declaration of Independence, threw up the first spadeful of dirt for the Baltimore and Ohio Railroad.

On the same day, July 4, 1828, President Adams opened the Chesapeake and Ohio Canal, which was to connect with the existing Potomac Canal, built by George Washington, at the Maryland–District of Columbia line.

At 8:00 A.M., a huge deputation met at the Union Hotel in Georgetown—the President and directors of the canal company, the mayors of Washington, Georgetown and Alexandria, committees from various corporations, heads of governmental departments, foreign ministers and a few invited guests. A band played as the group boarded the steamboat *Surprise*, which carried them to the Potomac Canal entrance. There a crowd of spectators had already gathered.

The president of the canal company gave a short address, then handed John Quincy a spade with which to throw up the first dirt. The veteran gardener plunged it confidently into the earth, only to meet stern resistance from a tree root. He struck again and again without making any headway. He became acutely aware of the watching multitude. The sun, now nearly overhead, burned through his heavy frock coat. Flushed and irritated, he stripped it off and threw it aside.

Then the shirtsleeved President plunged the spade into the ground and came up with a shovelful of dirt. A triumphant shout rang out as John Quincy turned to resume his coat and deliver his address.

"I've never shone as a public performer," John Quincy told Louisa that evening, "but today I was a huge success!"

That fall, Andrew Jackson won a clear majority at the polls. The Democrats had carried on a heated campaign throughout the four years of Adams' Administration, while he so consistently refused to be a political time-server that he would not even turn out of office avowed Jackson men who were working against him. Yet 44 per cent of the nation still voted for John Quincy Adams.

"If you would only campaign and use patronage to save yourself," the more realistic Clay and Webster told him repeatedly.

"I do not know how," he replied, and they knew it was so.

On a February evening in 1829, the President's Mansion shone with myriad candles in every room. Strains of music drifted on the cold air from the great north door which stood open to admit the stream of guests. In the Oval Room, the

President and the First Lady, with members of the Cabinet and their ladies, stood to receive them. Louisa was erect in her straight gown which fell in gracefold folds from its high sash. Her few jewels shone against the pallor of her skin. Not a trace of gray showed in her chestnut curls piled high on her lovely head. Her smile was cordial and she made small talk with everyone.

"I shall take the Adams' ship out with all flags flying," she had vowed to her niece as they prepared for the last reception. Mary Catherine was now an Adams too, having married John the year before. The last months in the Executive Mansion had been brightened by the birth of their daughter, Mary Louisa, now two months old.

John Quincy felt no compulsion to be gracious. He hurried his guests along to the Green and Yellow Rooms on either side of the Oval Room, where liveried servants passed trays of cakes and liqueurs, light wines, tea or coffee.

"The only thing I shall really miss is the garden," he declared when the farewell reception was over, "especially Owsley's double-blossomed peaches."

Owsley was the official gardener, a fixture at the White House. John Quincy was forced to leave behind the faithful Antoine and his English wife as well. In retirement, he could no longer afford their services.

The first months of leisure were spent in a rented mansion on Meridian Hill, a nearby suburb of Washington. Louisa's health did not improve, so in April, John Quincy decided to send her to the deeper solitude of Quincy. John had taken over the management of the Columbian Mills near Rock Creek, in which his father had recently invested, and Charles Francis was starting practice in Boston, so George was summoned to take his mother home.

On May 2 came news that the young man had disappeared during the night from the steamboat, *Benjamin Franklin*. He was lost without trace somewhere in Long Island Sound.

Louisa became hysterical with grief. Her mind wandered back to the happy days in Berlin when she had held her first-born in her arms. Over and over she cried: "Why? How could such a thing happen? His future was so promising!"

Leaving her with Mary Catherine, the heartbroken father traveled to New York with John to discover what they could. George's body had been recovered near City Island, but John Quincy could not bring himself to view it. All that was left to him were a few pitiful effects—a silver pencil, comb and snuffbox, a penknife, some small change and a watch. The hands had stopped at 3:40.

John returned to his wife and mother and the mill, while his father continued on to Boston with George's coffin. Charles Francis and Thomas met him there.

"In going over George's papers," Charles Francis reluctantly informed his father, "I find he had made a dreadful muddle of your affairs which he was handling. I believe he hoped to straighten things out before seeing you, but he was deep in debt. The poor fellow had wound himself nearly up in his own net!"

No one voiced the thought that was in all their minds: "Could George have committed suicide?"

John Quincy's mind rejected the thought, while his heart echoed Louisa's anguished question: "Why?"

When George's debts were paid, there was little left to repair the mansion at Quincy, which had been neglected since John Adams' death. John Quincy and Charles Francis camped out in the empty rooms, worked in the garden, swam in the creek. With Thomas and his son, Thomas, Jr., they went over

John Adams' papers preparatory to writing his memoirs. After a suitable time, neighbors invited them to chowder suppers and clambakes on the beach. Charles Francis persuaded his father to attend.

"There is someone I wish you to meet," he coaxed.

The someone was Miss Abigail Brooks whom Charles Francis married that September. John Quincy returned to Louisa in Washington with happy details of the wedding to divert her from her sorrow.

Slowly the months of leisure mended John Quincy's battered spirit. He had time, at last, to read and attend the theater. He had time to talk with callers on subjects other than politics.

"The ex-President was the chief talker," wrote one gentleman. "He spoke with infinite ease, drawing upon his vast resources with certainty. The whole of the conversation, which steadily he maintained for nearly four hours, was a continued stream of light . . . on the architecture of the Middle Ages, sculpture, poets and playwriters. . . ."

In Washington, legislators of every party climbed Meridian Hill to confer with the former President. Even Secretary of State Martin Van Buren, who had been a severe critic of the Adams Administration, became a regular caller, as was John Quincy's lifelong friend, John Marshall, Chief Justice of the Supreme Court.

"My life for the public is closed," John Quincy confided to the aging judge as they walked in the garden one autumn afternoon. "I only hope to make the remainder useful to my family and neighbors."

The white-haired Justice laughed. "An old war horse like you cannot be through at sixty-three, John. But I cannot remain much longer on the bench. By the way, I will rule for the Cherokees and the Creeks in their case against Georgia. I agree with you and Governor Barbour that they have a right to the land they occupy and the Indian nations should be considered a separate political community."

John Quincy shook his head. "I fear theirs is a lost cause, even with a strong champion like yourself. I fear more the defiant attitude of Georgia—and of other states—toward federal law."

A new threat to the Union clouded the horizon. The state of South Carolina, led by Vice-President John Calhoun himself, was threatening to "nullify" federal tariff laws.

"Our fathers won independence," John Quincy mused, "but the battle for a strong Union may outlive us."

In September, 1830, while John Quincy was making his annual visit to Quincy, a deputation of neighbors, including political leaders and newspaper editors of Plymouth County, called on him. Would he, their spokesman asked, be willing to serve his home district in Congress?

"Now really, Father," Charles Francis remonstrated when John Quincy announced he would accept the nomination. "There is no benefit to either of us to be always struggling before the public without rest or intermission!"

"No person could be degraded by serving the people as representative in Congress," John Quincy reprimanded his youthful critic. "If the people elected me town selectman, I would consider it an honor."

He did not remind his son that the eight dollars a day he would receive as congressman would be a welcome adjunct to his pension. In Washington, he and Louisa had moved into John's small home. The mills were not doing well, and John Quincy was in debt to Antoine, who was now proprietor of a successful restaurant. The independent Belgian had put up with President Jackson's violent temper for only a few months before leaving his employ to go into business for himself. He had pressed his old friend and benefactor to share his good fortune.

"Without your help, Monsieur," he told John Quincy, "I should still be a houseboy in Ghent."

The people of John Quincy's home district gave him an overwhelming vote that November that was more gratifying to him than his election as President. On Independence Day the following summer, before taking his seat in Congress, the former President threw down the gauntlet before those who sought to destroy the pact made fifty-five years before between the states. He declared:

> The Declaration of Independence was a social compact, by which the whole people covenanted with each citizen of the United Colonies, and each citizen with the whole people. . . . To this compact, union was as vital as freedom or independence. It is now the claim for one state of this Union, by virtue of her sovereignty, not only to make, but to unmake, the laws of the twenty-four, each equally sovereign with her.
> ". . . were this my last breath," he proclaimed, "my expiring words to you and your children should be, *independence and union forever!*"

On December 5, 1831, John Quincy Adams, sixty-four years old, took his seat in the Twenty-second Congress of the United States. When he entered the Hall of Representatives, the assembled legislators rose in silent tribute to their newest, their most distinguished and their oldest member. His most inveterate enemies came to shake his hand in welcome.

Representative Adams' first official act was the presentation of fifteen petitions from citizens of Pennsylvania praying for the abolition of slavery and of the slave trade in the District of Columbia. He ignored the established practice of dispensing with the reading of such petitions, and moved that one be read.

"I cannot personally support that part of the petition that prays for the abolition of slavery in the district," he remarked, and moved that they all be referred to the committee on the District of Columbia.

When the House adjourned, a member of the Society of Friends from Pennsylvania came down from the gallery to speak to Mr. Adams.

"We sent our petitions to you because we felt you were sympathetic to our cause," he reproached the elderly congressman.

"I abhor slavery," Congressman Adams assured the good Friend. "My family have never owned slaves and I am proud to come from the only state in the Union whose very first census of population in 1790 returned in the column for slaves —none. However," he continued kindly, "I do not think that the inhabitants of one state are competent to petition the legislature on a matter so deeply affecting the interests of another. A discussion of this issue could only stir up ill blood without accomplishing anything—at this time."

The tariff was, however, a matter of federal income affecting all the states. President Jackson asked Congress to issue a "force bill" authorizing him to use the army and navy to enforce federal law in South Carolina. John Quincy watched with interest the bill's progress through the House, since this was the very power he had asked in the controversy between Georgia and the Indians.

At the same time, President Jackson asked for a new tariff, a task referred to the House committee on manufactures, of which former President Adams was chairman. The tariff that emerged passed both Houses and was signed by the President on July 14, 1832. South Carolina accepted the "Adams Tariff" as the new bill was quickly named—then nullified the "force" bill.

"So South Carolina has the last word," John Quincy exclaimed to Henry Clay and Edward Everett, who as senators had conferred with him on the new tariff. "And the cancer remains and grows. Union or disunion—state or nation."

15

★★★★★★★★★★★★★★★★★★★★ **15** ★★★★★★★★★★★★★★★★★★★★

"Am I Gagged, Sir?"

When John Quincy went into the House of Representatives, Henry Clay had asked playfully: "How does it feel to turn boy and begin again?"

The veteran diplomat and statesman had to learn a new pattern of political thought. No vestige of Federalism remained, and Jefferson's Republicans had splintered into half a dozen segments, the largest being the Jacksonian Democrats. Their theory of "equal protection and equal benefits" heralded the flood tide of democracy.

He must learn to work with new men as those who had served the country since its birth passed from the scene. On Independence Day, 1831, James Monroe died at the home of his daughter, Mrs. Samuel Gouveneur, in New York. For years, John Quincy had always called on his aging chief when traveling between Washington and Quincy, so had watched sadly as the handsome former President wasted away.

In Virginia, James Madison survived three years more. His tiny body became so shriveled and bent with arthritis that he looked like a helpless bird perched midst his cushions. John Quincy drove out to see him often, but never saw him show a sign of the pain that must have racked his body. His eyes remained bright with that spirit that neither political opponent nor Britain's fleet had been able to intimidate.

The same year, word came from France that the Marquis de Lafayette was dead, and in 1835, John Marshall died in Philadelphia. During thirty years as Chief Justice, he had strengthened the Constitution and made the Supreme Court an effective arm of the federal government.

The years brought personal sorrow to John Quincy, too, with the loss of his younger brother, Thomas, in 1832, then of his second son, John, in 1834. Numb with grief, John Quincy carried out his duties that winter with difficulty. John had been his secretary and constant companion for over ten years.

While Louisa wept with her niece, John's widow, John Quincy consoled himself with John's little daughters. With infinite patience he helped five-year-old Mary Louisa spell out the words in her first reader, while he bounced the baby Georgiana on his knee.

That summer, he left them to tour the White Mountains with Charles Francis' wife, Abigail. In 1831, she had presented him with a granddaughter, Louisa Catherine, and, in September, 1833, she had produced a new John Quincy Adams. Though this trip was for her health, she remained unfailingly good-natured during the whole vacation.

Now he traveled between Quincy and Washington in the space of a day—by steamship and rail—a trip that had taken three weeks when he was a senator. That November he stopped over in New York as usual, then took the train from Amboy, New Jersey. The cars were replicas of the stage coaches, each with three private compartments. There were, as well, open platform cars with facing benches that could carry forty or fifty persons.

With characteristic curiosity, John Quincy timed the pace of the train as they sped across the flat Jersey farmlands towards Washington. They had just traversed a mile in one minute and thirty-six seconds according to his calculations when he was thrown abruptly to the left side of the car. Glancing around, he was startled to see the car behind climb up the rear of his, then overset to the right.

"This circumstance saved our car," he explained to Mary Catherine who, with Mary Louisa, met him at the station in Washington, "for the pressure to the right of the overset car brought the wheels of ours back onto the track. All but one person in the upset car were injured. The accident was caused by a wheel catching fire and sliding off the track. The train was going much too fast, of course. I believe we were going over forty miles an hour!"

Mary Louisa gripped her grandfather's hand and looked up at him earnestly. "You are my only Daddy now," she reminded him. "You must be careful."

John Quincy lifted the child and hugged her close so that she could not see the tears that blurred his eyes.

"They are tears of gratitude," he explained to Mary Catherine as the three walked along F Street toward the old home at Thirteenth, to which they had returned after John's death. "For each gap in my old heart made by the loss of a loved one, God in His Infinite Goodness has refilled."

Early in 1836, southern congressmen determined to block off antislavery petitions in Congress. In May, a special committee reported three proposed resolutions.

1. Congress has no constitutional power to interfere in any way with slavery in any of the states.

2. Congress ought not to interfere in any way with slavery in the District of Columbia.
3. All petitions, memorials, resolutions, propositions or papers relating in any way to the subject of slavery, shall be laid on the table, and no further action whatever shall be had thereon.

Speaker James K. Polk was a stanch Administration man and a Tennessee slaveholder. He recognized one southern member after another to speak on behalf of the resolutions, while northern members squirmed unhappily in their seats. Some looked hopefully at their most seasoned parliamentarian who surely could find some loophole in the resolutions. The aged member from Massachusetts was hunched over his desk, eyes closed. He might have been sleeping but for one telltale sign. His bald head appeared to gleam redder with each passing moment. Suddenly his veined hand clutched the desk. He pushed himself to his feet and asked the Chair to recognize him.

Speaker Polk quickly recognized another member who moved to discuss the previous question thus cutting off debate on the resolutions.

"Am I gagged or am I not?" demanded the former President.

"The motion for the previous question is not debatable," Speaker Polk pronounced.

Up to now John Quincy had not felt the time was right to bring the slavery battle into the open. That this divisive question must surely split the Union he had believed since the Missouri trouble. His own constituents were divided on the matter of slavery. But now the slave interests themselves had linked the issue of slavery with a direct violation of the

First Amendment to the Constitution—a matter that must be discussed.

When the first resolution came to a vote, John Quincy rose politely.

"If the House will allow me five minutes, I will prove the resolution untrue."

"Order! Order!" came cries from all over the House.

Speaker Polk passed Representative Adams to complete the roll call. Only eight other members voted against the resolution.

Before voting on the other two, the House resumed the regular order of the day—the discussion of relief rations for refugees of the Indian wars. On this apparently harmless subject, Speaker Polk gave Representative Adams the floor. The wily old legislator deftly turned the discussion to the general war powers of Congress.

War with Mexico threatened over her renegade province of Texas. When the alien government at Chapultepec outlawed slavery, the irate Texans revolted and were now soliciting union with the United States.

"Do you think antislavery England and France will stand by with folded arms while slavery is re-established in territory where it has been outlawed?" John Quincy demanded. "If we grab Texas for slavery, will not England take Cuba for freedom? Such a war might extend to the North American continent itself."

The members stirred uneasily. "What's the old madman leading up to?" whispered a young Georgian to his neighbor.

But even the Speaker was listening too intently to stop the Massachusetts member if he could.

"Mr. Chairman, are you ready for all these wars?" asked John Quincy, warming to his subject. "A Mexican war? A war with Great Britain if not with France? A general Indian war?" He felt the stimulus of the members' rapt, if not friendly, attention as he pointed a bony shaking finger toward the southern bloc. "Your own southern states must be the Flanders of these complicated wars, the battlefield upon which the last great conflict must be fought between slavery and emancipation!"

The words evoked the horrid spectre of slave insurrection in the silent aisles of Congress.

"Do you imagine that your Congress will have no constitutional authority to interfere with the institution of slavery in any way in the states of this confederation?"

The question hung like a pall, then was ripped by John Quincy's nasal voice, sharp as a blade:

"From the instant that your slaveholding states become the theater of war, civil, servile, or foreign—from that instant the war powers of Congress extend to interference with the institution of slavery in every way by which it can be interfered with."

The storm of protest rolled over Representative Adams. They were warned, at least. Their resolution was senseless.

When the vote was taken on the second resolution, John Quincy abstained, but when the roll call reached him on the third, he jumped to his feet and screamed, before they could silence him:

"I hold the resolution to be in direct violation of the Constitution of the United States, of the rules of this House, and of the rights of my constituents!"

Speaker Polk deliberately ignored the outburst, but the people did not. The "gag" rule as it came to be called, linked freedom of speech with abolition, and white men and women who had never given a thought to the plight of the Negro, became fearful for their own constitutional freedoms.

John Quincy's own Plymouth District—enlarged and renamed the Twelfth Congressional District—vibrated with historical echoes from Plymouth Rock. His constituents rallied solidly behind their ancient gladiator, sending him back to the arena year after year to fight for their rights. At the opening of every session, the stooped and trembling figure rose to challenge the ever-tightening gag—and was voted down. Day after day he doggedly presented his petitions, sometimes as many as two hundred in one day. He used every trick he knew to break the parliamentary stranglehold, while his exasperated opponents watched for opportunities to make a fool of him.

One day in February, 1837, John Quincy asked the Speaker, "May I present a paper purporting to be from slaves."

Before the paper could be sent to the Chair, the House rang with objections. Mr. Adams was "insulting the South, trifling with the Union!" Mr. Adams was "inciting slaves to rebellion!" Mr. Adams most certainly should be censured.

John Quincy quietly waited out the storm. Finally he reminded his attackers that he had only applied respectfully to the Speaker for a decision as to the propriety of such a petition. The reply of the House was a new set of resolutions denying slaves the right of petition "secured to the people of the United States by the Constitution."

John Quincy was on his feet immediately, demanding recognition. His bald head shone, his white side-whiskers shook with fury.

"What, sir?" he cried. "Will you put the right of petitioning, of craving for help and mercy and protection, on the footing of political privileges? . . . no despot has ever denied this humble privilege to the poorest or the meanest of human creatures. . . ."

After that, the Honorable Mr. Adams began getting a different sort of letter amongst the mass of petitions. Mary Catherine turned pale when she opened the first one. In bold black print, it declared:

"Vengeance is mine, say the South!" Below these words was an upraised blade and a whip. "Flog and Spare Not!"

"What does it mean, Uncle?" she asked.

"It means, my dear," John Quincy told her happily, "that my arrows are drawing blood. Don't tell your aunt about the letters," he warned.

It was too late. Louisa was already at the door, and heard Mary Catherine exclaim over another letter. Her aunt took it from her hand, and read:

"The rod is cut and seasoned that will make your old hide smart for your insidious attempt on southern rights."

Louisa pleaded tearfully with her husband to abandon the fight. "Charles Francis thinks it is unseemly for a man of your eminence to participate in political brawls of this sort!" she scolded, becoming so upset that she had to be put to bed. Before he went to the capital, John Quincy found another letter for her to read when she was calmer.

"Respected Man," wrote an admirer from Boston. "I know you will not fear to express your views, and it will have a tremendous effect in removing oppression and extending freedom. Go on then, Sage of Quincy! Fear not southern insolence. Defend our petitions and in turn we will defend and sustain you."

Not all John Quincy's legislative labors were stormy. In 1835 he was made chairman of a committee to report on an unusual bequest. An Englishman, James Smithson, an experimenter in the natural sciences, had left his entire fortune to the United States—"to found at Washington, under the name Smithsonian Institution, an Establishment for the increase and diffusion of knowledge among men."

President Jackson doubted the constitutionality of accepting such a gift from a foreigner. Most legislators still maintained that Congress had no power to establish a university or any other institution for the diffusion of knowledge. John Quincy considered the bequest a windfall and argued: "Intelligence is the exclusive attribute of man. Whoever increases his knowledge, multiplies the uses to which he is enabled to turn this gift of his Creator to his benefit."

The bequest, which amounted to a half-million dollars in United States currency, was accepted and invested in Arkansas state bonds. Year after year, debates continued over what was to be done with the fund. John Quincy clung to his desire for a national observatory, believing astronomy to be the most important of all the sciences. But his main concern was to keep the principal intact, and not allow it to be scattered here and there on minor projects. Eventually, in August of 1846, Congress enacted a bill creating The Smithsonian Institution.

With age, John Quincy had become such a facile orator that Congress had dubbed him their "Old Man Eloquent." When he rose to speak, members gathered magically from the corridors and antechambers to listen to the wisdom of the ancient statesman. By the same token, they had felt the whiplash of his tongue on the issues of slavery and petition, and took every means to shut him up or frighten him away from those subjects.

One day he found some two hundred black men waiting on the steps of the Capitol to hiss and boo at him.

"Send the Massachusetts Madman home!" they chanted.

With the help of the gold-headed cane recently given him by his grateful constituents, John Quincy laboriously climbed the steps till he could look down on the men. His blue eyes blazed young in his wrinkled kindly face.

"So you love your chains?" John Quincy asked softly. All the shrill combativeness that he reserved for his enemies on the floor was gone. The dark eyes in the ebony faces stared at him questioningly when he asked, "Who put you up to this?" He needed no other answer than those sad blank eyes.

Such incidents only succeeded in turning a parliamentary debate into a personal emotional issue. Others began occurring that involved John Quincy irretrievably.

One night as he walked home from the Capitol at dusk, a figure emerged from the shadow of a building. Involuntarily, the legislator's fingers closed more tightly on his cane. His weakening eyes could barely distinguish the raggy figure whose dark skin blended with the shadows.

"It's Nathan Allen, sir," the man said softly. "I saw you at the slave mart last week when they sold my wife and children south. Black folks say you is friend?"

"And what can I do for you, my friend?" John Quincy asked kindly. What must it be like, he thought, to see your loved ones sold into bondage, to be taken God knows where, to be separated, perhaps never to meet again in this life?

"Your little girl," he said aloud, "appeared to be about my granddaughter's age."

"Yes, sir," Allen replied, "she's eight. I told that man Birch who bought 'em that I'd buy my family back. See I got my freedom papers. Said he'd leave 'em here in jail for a week, but I don't know where I'll get so much money!"

John Quincy took Nathan Allen home and gave him fifty dollars as well as the names of sympathetic friends. "Come back before the week is up and tell me how much you have collected," he told the man, as he shuffled off down the walk. "We'll buy your family out of slavery at least," he added under his breath. As he turned, he saw Louisa standing in the drawing-room door. She was very pale, but she nodded understanding.

On a February day, in 1839, when he rose to make his routine protest against the "gag," he hurried on while he had the floor.

"My real position is not understood," he explained. "I earnestly advocate the right of petition according to the First Amendment to the Constitution. I earnestly defend the right of any man to be an abolitionist. The great men of the Revolution were all abolitionists."

"I object!" a member from Virginia shouted, but the Speaker called him to order.

"Any man, I say, has the right to petition for the abolition of slavery in the District of Columbia, or against the annexation of Texas, or anything else," Mr. Adams continued. "But I for one am not prepared to grant their prayer for abolition."

There was a rustle throughout the House, especially in the upper gallery which nowadays was filled with abolitionists come to hear their champion and give him moral support. John Quincy hurried on: "The abolition of slavery can only be accomplished by constitutional amendment. I therefore suggest the following amendments to the Constitution of the United States.

1. From and after the 4th day of July, 1842, there shall be throughout the United States, no hereditary slavery; but on and after that day every child born within the United States, their territories or jurisdiction, shall be born free.

2. With the exception of the Territory of Florida, there shall henceforth never be admitted into this Union any state, the constitution of which shall tolerate within the same the existence of slavery.

3. From and after the 4th of July, 1845, there shall be neither slavery nor slave trade at the seat of Government of the United States.

Shouts of "Order!" greeted the resolutions as if they were more petitions. Speaker Polk silenced the House in order to receive the amendments. John Quincy did not press the motion. He had gone on record before the country, the abolitionists, and before his God, to show the only way in which slavery could be abolished without violence or injustice—that is by constitutional amendment. He knew the House would not even consider his proposals.

16

★★★★★★★★★★★★★★★★★★★★ **16** ★★★★★★★★★★★★★★★★★★★★

"Stop the Music of John Quincy Adams!"

While John Quincy puttered amongst his seedlings that Indian summer, the coastal survey brig *Washington* took into custody the schooner *Amistad* and brought her into New London, Connecticut. Dock workers and customs officials in that whaling town were accustomed to exotic sailors but when this vagrant vessel disgorged her crew, a surprised crowd gathered.

Over thirty stocky Africans stepped ashore, followed by three pathetic female children and several sickly women. All wore a fantastic assortment of clothing. They spoke no recognizable language. Two irate Cubans were found locked below decks. They claimed the Negroes were slaves they had purchased in Cuba to work their sugar plantations on another island. In transit, the blacks had managed to cut their chains, murder the ship's captain and cook, and take possession of the vessel.

The federal marshal was not inclined to turn the pathetic group of Africans over to their furious Cuban masters. He secured the mutineers in the local jail and sent the owners off to Washington to put their case before the Spanish minister there.

The Spanish emissary demanded immediate return of the "property" to the owners and President Martin Van Buren was prepared to sign an executive order to that effect in order to avoid an international incident. The order met firm resistance from the free state of Connecticut, where authorities refused to release the captives without a fair trial.

But how could men be tried if they could utter not a single word in their own defense? None spoke Spanish, indicating, their protectors argued, that they could not have lived long in either Spain or Cuba. Were they, then, slaves, or free Africans, illegally transported from Africa? Spain as well as the United States and Britain had outlawed the international slave trade thirty years ago.

A Yale professor of languages, with the help of African seamen brought out from New York, soon picked up the word sounds of the strange tribe whom the sailors identified as Mendi from the northern border of Nigeria. Their leader, a handsome giant named Singbe-Piéh, whom the Spaniards called Cinque, quickly acquired enough English to fill in the details of their ordeal.

Over fifty of his tribe, he maintained, had been kidnapped from their village and sold from ship to ship off the coast of Guinea. Finally they had been taken across the big water to Cuba and auctioned off in the slave mart of Havana. When they were taken aboard the coastal schooner, the terrified children of the jungle seized their last hope of freedom. They killed the captain and the cook. The Cubans had been spared to navigate the ship back to Africa. By day they sailed the ship east, but at night the wily owners doubled back towards North America.

John Quincy watched with interest as the case was referred
from one court to another. Eminent lawyers gathered from
all the northern states of the Union and from Canada and
Great Britain to confer and plead for the Africans. The
Amistad case became a "cause célèbre" in the long battle
against slave smuggling. In 1840, the case was referred to the
United States Supreme Court. A young Connecticut lawyer,
Roger Baldwin, traveled to Quincy to persuade the eminent
Quincy lawyer and fighter for human rights to represent the
Negroes before the highest tribunal.

John Quincy hesitated. "I am seventy-four years old," he
reminded Baldwin, "—too old, too oppressed with my duties
in the House, too inexperienced, after thirty years, in the
forms and technicalities of arguments before the Supreme
Court."

But on February 22, 1841, John Quincy stood before the
Supreme Court tribunal for the first time in thirty-two years.
The small pie-shaped room was in the east wing of the Capitol
beneath the Senate chamber. On the rounded end was a row
of windows beneath which the judges sat. John Quincy's failing eyes grew red and watery as he strained against the light
to see the faces of the men on the bench. He was worried
about the case. Except for Justice Joseph Story of Marblehead, Massachusetts, the judges were all Jacksonian Democrats, most of them slaveholding southerners. He knew there
were already plots to smuggle the Africans to Canada if the
judgment went against them, rather than surrender the poor
souls to the untender mercies of a Cuban court.

The attorney for the government opened the case and
droned on for two hours: the slave property must be turned
over to Spain.

Next day John Quincy spoke for the defense. Word had

got around that the former President was to speak and the chamber galleries were packed.

Were the Africans slaves by the laws of Spain? That was the very issue.

"It is absurd to apply the fugitive slave laws of the United States to the outlawed transatlantic slave trade," he declared. "By Spain's own treaties with Great Britain the men in question were free men of an illegal cargo."

As the old contender spoke the infirmities of his years were forgotten. For four and a half hours, he blazed with righteous scorn and sarcasm, damning the executive power that would deliver resolute free men to the vengeance of foreign slaveholders.

On March 9, the court declared the Mendi captives free. The United States Supreme Court, at least, had gone on record before the world as the defender of free men.

But John Quincy's own battle in Congress continued against an ever-tightening gag. In 1840 a more stringent ruling, called the 25th rule, had been adopted.

No petition, memorial, resolution or other paper, praying for the abolition of slavery in the District of Columbia or any state or territory, or the slave trade between the states and territories of the United States in which it now exists, shall be received by this House, or entertained in any way whatsoever.

John Quincy's countermotion—that all petitions be received unless specific objection be made—was rejected.

"You seem to feel sore about the gag rule," a North Carolina member baited the old member from Massachusetts.

"I do," replied John Quincy, "but the mortification I feel is not for my own defeat, but for the disgrace and degradation of my own country, trampling to death the first principle of human liberty. This is the iron that enters into my soul. Yet, the faculties are dropping from me as the teeth are dropping from my head. What can I do?"

Already he had done much. In identifying the cause of antislavery with that of white freedom he had succeeded in breaking down party lines. Each year the margin by which the gag rule was passed narrowed. Southerners and their dwindling northern sympathizers were increasingly convinced that they must get rid of the "mischievous bad old man" before he started a positive antislavery movement in Congress.

On January 25, 1842, the Honorable Mr. Adams presented a petition so enormous in its implications that his adversaries were certain he himself had handed them the weapon that would destroy him. The memorial, from Haverhill, Massachusetts, asked that Congress immediately adopt "measures peaceably to dissolve the Union of these States."

"I move that the document be referred to a select committee which should be instructed to report an answer to the petitioners showing why their prayer should not be granted."

But his adversaries were already snapping at his heels.

"Is it in order," asked Henry Wise of Accomac, Virginia, who had for years taken every opportunity to discredit the "Old Harlequin" as he called John Quincy, "to move to censure any member presenting such a petition?"

"Good," John Quincy exclaimed from his seat, loud enough so that several startled members nearby heard him.

The question raised a babel of inquiries. John Quincy waited for the House to quiet before rising.

"I am surprised," he announced clearly, "that such an objection should come from a quarter where there have been so many calculations of the value of the Union."

Someone nervously moved to adjourn.

"I hope the House will not adjourn," declared its eldest member. "If there is to be a vote of censure, the House might as well settle the question now."

The House refused to adjourn, and another Virginian, Thomas Gilmer, put forth a motion for censure.

"I do not feel at liberty to arrest the proceeding," Speaker John White decided, and cited as precedent the immediate action of censure brought against the Honorable J. Q. Adams in 1836 when he had offered a petition from slaves.

"I hope this resolution will be received and debated," John Quincy urged, "and that I shall have the privilege of again addressing the House in my own defense—especially," he continued with measured sarcasm, "as the gentleman from Virginia has thought proper to play second fiddle to his colleague from Accomac."

Gilmer shouted in rage, "I play second fiddle to no man. I am endeavoring to stop the music of one 'Who, in the course of one revolving moon,/Was poet, fiddler, statesman, and buffoon.' "

Yes, stop the music of John Quincy Adams echoed the southern slaveholders. Stop his eternal trumpeting for freedom! He merited, they cried, expulsion from the national councils, the severest censure ". . . for conduct so utterly unworthy of his past position to the state, and his present position."

The final long resolution of censure was presented by Thomas Marshall of Kentucky, nephew of John Quincy's respected friend, former Supreme Court Justice John Marshall.

"The gentleman from Massachusetts has done nothing less

than invite members of the House to commit high treason," cried young Tom Marshall, "when he submitted a petition for the dissolution of the Union!"

"Sir," asked John Quincy, "where did you learn your law? Certainly not from your distinguished uncle. What is high treason? It is not for the gentleman from Kentucky, or his puny mind, to define what high treason is and confound it with what I have done. If the Clerk of the House will read the first paragraph of the Declaration of Independence . . ." He repeated his request so all could hear ". . . the first paragraph of the Declaration of Independence!"

The clerk began to drone out the immortal lines: "When in the course of human events, it becomes necessary for one people to dissolve the political bands which have connected them with another . . ."

"Proceed," cried John Quincy, "down to the 'right and duty.' "

The clerk droned on through the rights of life, liberty and the pursuit of happiness to the right and duty of free men after a long train of abuses to provide new safeguards for their future security.

"Now, sir," said the son of John Adams, "I rest the right of petition of the people of Haverhill on the Declaration of Independence. If that right, or any others are taken away by this coalition of southern slaveholders and northern democracy, it is time for the northern people to see if they can't shake it off. I can say that it is not yet time to do this. The other means have not been tried. I do say that if the petition is answered, it will satisfy the petitioners."

Again a confused and divided legislature withdrew the motion of censure.

John Quincy Adams, 2nd, was ten years old the summer of 1843 when he traveled with his mother and grandfather in the "cars" through the blooming countryside of western Massachusetts, through the dark forests and stupendous rocks of the Berkshires into the rich valley of the Hudson. From Saratoga they took the stage to Lake George and Lake Champlain and thence into Canada.

Coming back through Niagara, John Quincy and his grandson stood hand and hand and gazed with equal wonder at the mighty cataract. Together they climbed down a steep cliff to view the whirlpool, scrambling over the rocks to get a better view. Watching the old man and the boy, a member of the party remarked, "Oh, that we could take the engine out of the old 'Adams' and put it in a new hull!"

They visited the Tuscarora Indian reservation where the seventy-six-year-old statesman spoke to a silent attentive audience.

"They don't seem very frightening, Grandfather," young John Quincy said in a stage whisper.

A chief who stood on the platform nearby overheard.

"To my people," he told the boy, "your grandfather will always be the Great White Father, defender of our rights."

Millard Fillmore, a colleague of John Quincy's in Congress, escorted them to Buffalo where they received a royal welcome. All across New York crowds gathered at every station to greet their patriarch. At Utica the party stopped overnight to rest. As they breakfasted next morning, John Quincy was called out to meet a well-dressed colored man who stood upon the steps. Behind him was a group of children, and behind them several more men and women.

"Please forgive us for disturbing you," their spokesman addressed Congressman Adams politely. "We heard you were staying in the city, and my people felt compelled to see you. We wish to thank you for your devotion to the cause of human rights."

That autumn, John Quincy traveled west again, to lay the cornerstone of an observatory to be built by the Cincinnati Astronomical Society. The yearly debates in Congress over how to use the Smithson fund had stimulated interest in the science of astronomy. West Point established a small observatory in 1839, and another was erected at Philadelphia the following year. In 1842, Congress voted funds for a building intended eventually to house a naval observatory, a project that finally fulfilled John Quincy's desire for such a government-run research station to probe the universe.

The trip to Ohio in the autumn of 1843 turned into another triumphal tour. Everywhere the people spoke to him, and their voice was the voice of love.

"Welcome, John Quincy Adams, Defender of the Rights of Man," read banners strung across his route.

After the ceremony at Cincinnati, the Adams party swung south into Kentucky for the trip home. In that border state men, women and children, black and white, lined his route. The men uncovered their heads as he passed between them.

John Quincy was close to tears himself. His lifelong dream seemed to be coming true. He was, at last, the Man of the Whole Country.

17

★★★★★★★★★★★★★★★★★★★★ **17** ★★★★★★★★★★★★★★★★★★★★

"The People Weep"

> When a Patriarch is removed,
> The people weep . . .

At the opening of the Twenty-eighth Congress in 1844, the 25th Standing Rule, known as the "Gag," was not renewed because of insufficient backing. On that day, John Quincy heard a colleague deliver on the floor of the House an impassioned indictment of slavery. No one had the right stop him.

"Blessed, ever blessed, be the name of God!" Tears of joy flowed unheeded from the old gladiator's rheumy eyes down the furrows of his cheeks. "The seals are broken. The door is open!"

In Massachusetts, Charles Francis had persuaded the legislature to draw up a constitutional amendment abolishing the two-thirds provision giving slaveowners representation for their slaves. Three times that year it was presented to Congress and rejected. Such an amendment could not yet pass the national legislature because it required a two-thirds majority in both Houses as well as three-fourths of the states. But John Quincy thought he heard the knell of doom for the South's "peculiar" institution.

In 1846, Texas was annexed to the United States. As the country moved toward war with Mexico, President James Polk already eyed covetously her California territories. John Quincy opposed the "most unrighteous war" to the end. He agreed with the Administration, however, that the acquisition of Oregon was "manifest destiny," as the United States served notice on Great Britain that the boundary must be settled.

That June 15, Secretary of State James Buchanan signed the treaty that fixed the boundary at the forty-ninth parallel. John Quincy's lifelong battle to hold that line in the Far West was finally realized.

The following month he entered his eightieth year. Washington was a sweltering 84° the morning of his birthday as he walked along Tiber Creek just after dawn. There was a bridge now across to the islet where he used to swim and three young men were already enjoying the cool water.

"There's John Quincy Adams!" cried one. The legislator smiled and raised his gold-headed cane in salute.

He walked on along the river bank toward the Potomac Bridge, a shuffling bent old man to the watching youths. Once out of sight, he turned to be certain he was alone.

"Every man to his own rock," he thought, as he peeled off his clothes and waded into the water.

That November he personally acknowledged the unanimous nomination of the Whig Convention of the Eighth District. In a voice so thin and tired that few people could hear him, he reminded his constituents that he had approved the notice to Great Britain over Oregon, but opposed the war with Mexico. His fellow citizens were satisfied. They returned him to Congress with a generous majority of votes.

Cold weather had already chased Louisa back to Washington accompanied by Mary Catherine and Mary Louisa. John

Quincy was staying with Charles Francis and his family in their gracious home at 57 Mount Vernon Street on Beacon Hill in Boston. The autumn visit had become a pleasant custom. This year another new baby warmed the house—a girl named Mary, the young Adams' fifth child.

On November 20, John Quincy took his early morning walk with an old friend, Dr. George Parkman, who wished to show him the new Harvard medical college. As they approached the bridge to Cambridge, the congressman stumbled and fell forward on one knee. Dr. Parkman caught him, breaking the fall.

"I feel a strange lightheaded weakness," John Quincy explained.

Dr. Parkman helped his companion home and put him to bed. A slight cerebral hemorrhage was his diagnosis.

Louisa hurried back from Washington to tend him. She traveled alone by rail and steamer, an unprecedented adventure for her.

"There is no pain," her husband assured her, "but I have little power for thought."

He spent the hours of rest drafting his will. By Christmas he was on his feet again, and on February 12 he returned to Congress. All the members rose to greet him, and proceedings were interrupted while two colleagues conducted him to his seat. Now when he spoke the words were blurred and feeble, so they had to gather near to understand him. But his bald head still grew red as a beacon when he disapproved of proceedings. He attended every session faithfully as ever, though he gave up all committees except the library.

That summer of 1847, John Quincy and Louisa traveled to Quincy earlier than usual to celebrate their golden wedding anniversary on July 26. Theirs had been a good life together, they agreed, often stormy, sometimes tragic, yet thrice blessed, then blessed again.

John's widow, Mary Catherine, had been their constant companion since her mother's death. Her daughter, Mary Louisa, now twenty, had filled the niche in their hearts left empty by the death of their only girl. John Quincy had taught his granddaughter to read, and supervised her education as he had his sons'.

Charles Francis and Abigail came down from Boston, and their children made the old mansion ring with laughter. Louisa Catherine was now a dignified sixteen, while John Quincy, 2nd, at fourteen, lorded it over twelve-year-old Charles Francis, Jr., and ten-year-old Henry. Beside the hearth, Louisa rocked the baby Mary in the old wooden cradle—the same in which Nabby rocked Thomas, John Quincy remembered with surprise.

Early in the first session of the Thirtieth Congress, John Quincy's old eyes came to rest on an extraordinary figure seated at the back of the Whig section. Many members were eccentric in manner or dress, but the elderly statesman from Massachusetts thought he had never seen a congressman who had quite so outlandish an appearance.

"Who is the new fellow," he asked the member next to him.

"Oh, he's from Illinois," was the reply. "Quite a rube. All the members find him amusing. Shall I introduce you?"

"By all means," John Quincy agreed.

The member from Illinois was impossibly tall. The sleeves of his top coat did not quite cover his bony wrists, and his ill-fitting trousers were held too high by suspenders. The Honorable John Quincy Adams had never seen such an ugly face—craggy and weatherbeaten, like the country whence he came: "Though he can hardly be forty years old," John Quincy surmised.

Then his uncertain vision focused on the man's eyes. They were dark, piercing, bottomless with intelligence.

"Mr. Adams, sir, may I present Mr. Abraham Lincoln of Illinois."

John Quincy placed his veined and shrunken hand into the huge hand extended to him. Mr. Lincoln's grip was gentle but firm and his voice had a soft quality that belied the rough exterior.

"This is a great honor, sir," the big westerner said. "I have been following your battle for the right of petition." Abraham Lincoln was staring fascinated at this patriarch of politics with his snowy sideburns and soft mouth, drawn now in a severe line. Beneath their reddened lids, the blue eyes were alert, searching and curious as those of a much younger person, warm with compassion.

"I find your views on slavery most interesting, sir," Mr. Lincoln continued, enduring the old man's scrutiny with poise, "and your defense of the Africans was fine—just fine!"

"There is much yet to be done," John Quincy mumbled, but Mr. Lincoln heard and understood.

At midmorning on Monday, February 21, John Quincy's carriage called to take him to the Capitol. He had not attempted the walk since his stroke. Before the session he chatted amiably with several other members. Resolutions were presented that morning for tendering thanks and decorations to several generals for gallant actions during campaigns of the Mexican War. As the clerk read the texts, Representative Adams' bald head grew crimson.

". . . splendid victories of our armies . . . scattering the armies of Mexico like chaff before the wind . . . crowned by possession of the far-famed Halls of Montezuma . . ."

A reporter sittting at the press table fifteen feet away noticed Mr. Adams' flushed appearance.

"He'll never vote for that string of lurid exaggerations!" thought Mr. Stanton of the Boston *Emancipator and Republican.*

The Speaker began to call the roll for a vote. John Quincy's name was third. He was anxious to voice a protest, but as he rose to his feet, a strange numbness suffused his body. He slumped forward on his desk. David Fisher of Ohio who sat beside him, caught the old man before he fell to the floor.

"Mr. Adams is dying," cried Washington Hunt of New York—but John Quincy did not hear.

An attendant brought cloaks from the cloakroom in which to wrap the stricken member, while another summoned a doctor. When John Quincy remained unconscious, members carried him to the Speaker's chamber where he was made comfortable on a couch. Rather than disturb him again, other doctors were called to tend him there. Despite their combined efforts, the old legislator showed no flicker of life other than an almost imperceptible heartbeat.

Louisa, nearly prostrated by worry and grief, came to see her husband each day supported by her niece and granddaughter—and went away again. Her beloved did not know her. Henry Clay came and, weeping, took his old friend's hand, but there was no answering pressure. The House stood adjourned and Washington Birthday celebrations were canceled as friend and foe alike kept a silent vigil outside the Speaker's chamber and throughout the city. Finally came Charles Francis who had hurried down from Boston, and he, too, went away to comfort his distraught mother.

At 7:20 P.M. on February 23, the old man stirred.

"I thank the officers of the House," John Quincy said in a muffled blurred tone. Then clearly, "This is the end of earth, but I am composed."

Louisa was sent for—but when she came, he was gone.

"A Patriarch has gone to rest," read the call to public mourning, published in Washington, "a link between the past and the present generation is broken—a Sage has fallen at his post!"

They laid him in a silver-mounted coffin decorated with a spread-winged eagle. Daniel Webster wrote the inscription.

JOHN QUINCY ADAMS
BORN
an inhabitant of Massachusetts
July 11, 1767
DIED
A citizen of the United States, in the
Capitol, at Washington, February 23, 1848,
Having served his country for half a century,
And enjoyed its highest honors.

For two days the people filed past to pay last homage to the Sage of Quincy. The funeral procession at Washington and memorial services elsewhere throughout the country assumed the proportions of a national pageant. Then they took John Quincy home to rest with his parents in the churchyard at Quincy.

As the funeral train made its halting way north, weeping crowds met it at every station, and stood in the frozen fields to watch it pass.

Henry Clay rode with John Quincy Adams on his last journey home, as did the incongruous congressman from

Illinois, Mr. Abraham Lincoln, a member of the House Committee on Arrangements. John C. Calhoun of South Carolina, who had been opposed to much for which John Quincy stood, helped carry him to the grave. For the moment, political differences were forgotten as the nation joined in tribute to the Massachusetts patriot.

★★

Bibliography

Adams, Henry. *Degradation of the Democratic Dogma*. New York: The Macmillan Co., 1919.

Adams, James Truslow. *The Adams Family*. New York: Blue Ribbon Books, 1930.

Adams, John Quincy. *Amistad Case*. New York: S. W. Benedict, 1841.

———. *Life in a New England Town*. Boston: Little, Brown & Co., 1903.

———. *Memoirs*. Philadelphia: J. B. Lippincott & Co., 1874.

Bemis, Samuel Flagg. *John Quincy Adams and the Foundations of American Foreign Policy*. New York: Alfred A. Knopf, Inc., 1949.

———. *John Quincy and the Union*. New York: Alfred A. Knopf, Inc., 1956.

Bobbé, Dorothie. *Mr. and Mrs. John Quincy Adams, an Adventure in Patriotism*. New York: Minton, Blach & Co., 1930.

Bowen, Catherine Drinker. *John Adams and the American Revolution*. Boston: Little, Brown & Co., 1950.

Clark, Bennett Champ. *John Quincy Adams: "Old Man Eloquent."* Boston: Little, Brown & Co., 1932.

Dumas, Alexandre. *Adventures in Czarist Russia*. Philadelphia and New York: Chilton Company, 1960.

Everett, Edward. *The Monroe Doctrine*. New York: W. C. Bryant & Co., 1863.

Holland, Janice. *They Built a City: The Story of Washington, D. C.* New York: Charles Scribner's Sons, 1958.

James, Marquis. *The Life of Andrew Jackson*. Indianapolis: The Bobbs-Merrill Company, 1938.

Marx, Rudolph. *Health of the Presidents*. New York: G. P. Putnam's Sons, 1960.

Minnigerode, Meade. *Some American Ladies*. New York: G. P. Putnam's Sons, 1926.

Nevins, Allan, ed. *The Diary of John Quincy Adams, 1794–1845*. New York: Charles Scribner's Sons, 1939.

Sandburg, Carl. *Abraham Lincoln, the Prairie Years*. New York: Harcourt, Brace & Co., 1939.

Tucker, Captain Samuel. *The Log of the Boston*. Boston: Massachusetts Historical Society, 1954.

Whitney, Janet Payne. *Abigail Adams*. Boston: Little, Brown & Co., 1947.

Whitton, Mary Ormsbee. *First First Ladies, 1789–1865*. New York: Hastings House, 1948.

Wilkie, Katharine E. *The Man Who Wouldn't Give Up: Henry Clay*. New York: Julian Messner, Inc., 1961.

Index

188

About the Author

Mary Hoehling was born in Worcester, Massachusetts, attended school there and in Noroton, Connecticut. After two years at Wheaton College, she left to marry and settle in Washington, D. C. Her first published "work" was a poem about a windswept beach which she wrote at the age of twelve and was published in the school paper. As she went through school, historic events and personalities captured her imagination, and when her children began complaining of the dullness of history in textbooks, she decided to try her hand at writing biography. She is married to the well known author, A. A. Hoehling, and is herself the author of several biographies for young people.